INTRODUCTION TO THE SPIRITIST PHILOSOPHY

WHAT IS SPIRITISM?

SPIRITISM: IN ITS SIMPLEST EXPRESSION

ALLAN KARDEC

First Edition (Christian Spiritism), 1985
Second Edition, (Introduction to the Spiritist Philosophy) 2004
Copyright © 2004

Published by:
Allan Kardec Educational Society
P.O. Box 26336
Philadelphia, PA 19141
Phone/Fax (215) 329-4010
www.allan-kardec.org
email: akesbooks@cox.net

The Allan Kardec Educational Society is a volunteer-run, nonprofit organization. Its officers receive no financial compensation.

Main entry under title:
Introduction to the Spiritist Philosophy
1. Spiritual Life 2. Human Development
3. Paranormality 1. Kardec, Allan, 1804

Library of Congress Catalog Card Number 2004094246
ISBN 0-9649907-7-6

(Translated from *Qu'Est-Ce Que Le Spiritisme?* (1865) and *Spiritisme Reduit a sa plus Simple Expression* (1865)

Printed in the United States of America.

In Memory

Benjamin Rodriguez
(1923-2001)

TABLE OF CONTENTS

CHAPTER II
ELEMENTARY PRINCIPLES OF THE SPIRITIST DOCTRINE

CHAPTER III
SOLUTION TO SOME PROBLEMS OF PHILOSOPHY

PART II—
SPIRITISM: IN ITS SIMPLEST EXPRESSION

PART III— BIOGRAPHICAL SKETCH

GLOSSARY

PREFACE TO THE ENGLISH EDITION

When this book appeared in France in 1865, Europe was in the midst of great revolutions. Darwin's *Origin of the Species*, published in 1859 was a scientific 'revelation' that changed how we saw ourselves, life, and God's role in the biology of life. Almost every area of intellectual endeavor was affected by the winds that were blowing from England. As the history of science testifies, some breakthrough ideas made their way through simultaneous interpreters, as if born in some transcendental field of inquiry. This was the case with the mechanism of natural selection which Charles Darwin and Alfred R. Wallace arrived at simultaneously by different routes.

The Spiritist philosophy, we dare to argue, was a variant born from that same transcendental field. In 1857, therefore, two years before The Origin of Species, the Spiritist Doctrine came to light offering a framework to explain humanity's purpose and destiny, which rests solidly upon the same concept of evolution. In so doing, it pulled God out of the churches and brought God to the fields, oceans, and cities where the human soul works, learns, and grows. The Spiritist Doctrine was the spearhead of another revolution, this time a revolution of the human spirit.

This book is, for all purposes, a primer on the Spiritist Doctrine. It contains two of Allan Kardec's works: *Qu'Est-Ce Que Le Spiritisme?* (What is Spiritism?) and *Spiritisme Reduit a sa plus Simple Expression* (Spiritism in its Simplest Expression). In the first work, Allan Kardec converses informally with three characters, a critic, a skeptic, and a priest, introducing them to a view of life and spirituality centered on the individual. The characters represent a composite of the adversarial stances Allan Kardec faced in Europe at a time when religious orthodoxy cast a dense shadow over people's views of reality. It is a light and engaging review of the Spiritist proposal detailed earlier in *The Spirits' Book*. The second work, though smaller in size, presents an insightful yet rich summary of the Spiritist wisdom. Less descriptive and more inspirational, it is a soulful letter addressed to the heart of the reader.

Contrary to the connotation that the word doctrine may have in many circles, the Spiritist Doctrine is not a conventional, ordinary religion. It does not have religious officers, rituals, or a tradition grown around sacred texts. It does not have a founder who has been visited by God, nor dispositions on worship of deity. It is therefore, not a religion in the external sense. It is, however, and it must be stressed here, a religion when we consider as religion the inner experience of the individual with the divine. In this realm of experience, a person's feelings, aspirations, and dreams are fueled with a different vitality, and in solitude the person bares the conscience before the divine. It is this expanded feeling that defines the religious aspect of the Spiritist Doctrine. The enlightened spirits who shaped the Spiritist philosophy have passionately encouraged this pursuit, for this is the essential religion of the soul.

This book will be more valuable to you in proportion to your desire to learn the Truth about the marvelous and mysterious universe that is our home. As Truth is and will always be relative (to our state of progress), joy will be the sweet fruit of journeying toward it. Billions of people on this plane have been convinced that their eternal destiny will be determined by what they believe. Their future is made to depend on their unquestionable acceptance of certain articles of religious dogma. This is called 'saving faith.' The Spiritist Doctrine defends that the truth is revealed equally in the Hebrew Bible, the Gospels, Quran, Bhagavad-Gita, Tao Te Ching and is revealed continuously in the discoveries of science, in the beauty of art and poetry, and in the courageous achievements of love. Ultimately, the spiritual voices have taught, how we live and what we apply our lives to is what really counts for our peace and fulfillment.

In order to establish a point of reference for the journey, Allan Kardec queried the enlightened voices about who was the most perfect example that God offered to us as a guide and model. Their answer was incisive: Jesus. Jesus is the model of moral perfection toward which we should all strive. While all the great beings and avatars lived in communion with the Divine, Jesus was, in their advice, the standard after which we should plan our spiritual journey. In a pure and non-sectarian way, we are Christians, since we are inspired by Jesus. In the same manner, a Muslim, Jewish, or Hindu person may be inspired by Christ's message. We drink eagerly from the fountain of His teachings, and deem the personal effort to live by the Gospel as the supreme task of a Spiritist person. In a dogma-free sense, Spiritists march gratefully under Christ's standard.

Many people gave their time and dedication to the publishing of this book. They are too many to fairly list all the names. They have contributed in so many different ways to make this publication possible and have done so as a way of sharing the light that already illuminates their souls. We are thankful to every one of you.

The Translation and Editorial Team
Philadelphia, 2004

Allan Kardec Educational Society

WHAT IS SPIRITISM?

PREFACE

Persons with only a passing familiarity with the Spiritist Doctrine are naturally, inclined to formulate certain questions whose answers may require an extra reading effort. In addition, they may not have the time and desire to devote themselves to a methodical research of the phenomena. Before engaging in this task, many want to know what it's all about and whether they want to pursue a more in-depth study. That is why we found it useful to present, in an abbreviated form, answers to some of the questions most often asked. In so doing, we hope to save the interested reader precious time and save us from repeating ourselves.

The first chapter of this volume presents, in a dialogue form, answers to the more common arguments raised by those who have yet a limited exposure to the fundamental principles of the Doctrine. It also addresses some of the more noteworthy arguments put forth by adversaries.

The second chapter is devoted to a summary exposition of the experimental aspects of this discipline. It focuses on the concepts that inform the mediumistic process. It will provide the reader with assistance to make a more informed judgment. This chapter is, approximately, a summary of *The Mediums' Book*. Objections are sometimes born from hasty judgment based on incomplete information. It is the goal of this section to provide ample information to satisfy most of these objections.

The third chapter might be considered an abstract of *The Spirits' Book*. It contains the answers, from a psychological, moral, and philosophical point of view to a number of problems to which no philosophy has yet given satisfactory answers. The structure furnished by the Spiritist Doctrine, when contrasted with other theories, will stand out for its sensibleness and rationality

These summaries are not only useful to beginners, who will be able in a short time and with little effort to acquire the essential notions of the Spiritist Doctrine, they are also useful to the more versed as they furnish the means to answer the objections that will undoubtedly come. Further, they may serve as reminders of points that should be held in high esteem by all.

To answer the question, "What is Spiritism?" proposed in the title, we suggest that:

> *Spiritism is, simultaneously, a philosophy and a field of scientific study. As a scientific endeavor, it studies the relationships between the physical and the spiritual worlds. As a philosophy, it deals with the moral implications of such relationships.*[1]

More explicitly, I advance that:

> *Spiritism is a science*[2] *that deals with the nature, origin, and destiny of spirits and their relation with the corporeal world.*

■ ■ ■

[1] *Translator's Note: The differences in usage of the word 'science' between the Eighteenth and Twentieth Centuries must not be ignored. Besides, the word has had an elastic meaning and was employed in the Eighteenth Century with a certain degree of freedom. Allan Kardec employed the word 'science' to primarily "denote the application of scientific methods in a field of study previously open only to theories based on subjective, historical, or undemonstrable abstract criteria." It should not, therefore, be confounded with the meaning that is dominant today, i.e., as synonymous with natural and physical science and the scientific empiricism that is their characteristic. The class of phenomena that is the object of the Spiritist Doctrine cannot be verified by the empirical methods of modern natural science. The Oxford English Dictionary was used as reference for this explanation.*

■ ■ ■

[2] *Translator's Note: The phenomena that are the subject of these dialogues are the same that the religious history of humankind witnessed in the life of the great mystical individuals. St. Paul had visions, heard voices, and on several occasions attended services in which disciples spoke in trance. St. Francis Assisi was guided by the Voice. St. Theresa d'Avila, possibly the greatest of all sensitives, heard voices, experienced visions, spoke*

Continues on page 13

Continued from page 12

in trance, and wrote in automatic trance. Outside of the church circle, but equally startling, was William Blake's testimony that he was 'under the direction of messengers from heaven, daily and nightly.' The Spiritist theory supports the notion that psychic sensitivity is an inherent faculty of human beings. Communication with the spirit world is a complex and challenging endeavor that requires discernment, elevated moral principles and intention, and dedication. The field of music offers a workable analogy. The masses love music, but only a small percentage of the people can read notes and play an instrument. A smaller percentage play an instrument well, just a few are virtuosos, and a handful approach creative genius. In the psychic area, the great mystics are the geniuses who enjoy the highest level of communion with divinity. The Spiritist philosophy, by analogy, is an experiential curriculum that prepares individuals to manifest their gift, master its potential, and play it well. A good medium, like a good musician, comes to be so only through consistent practice, personal dedication, love for the art, and an extra quota of compassion for all beings. In mediumship, as in music, skill and talent vary ad infinitum.

CHAPTER I

FIRST DIALOGUE

THE CRITIC

Visitor   I admit that I can't accept the reality of the strange phenomena attributed to spirits. I believe spirits are imaginary. But I would be convinced if I were given
unquestionable proof of their existence. Therefore, I
want to attend one or two experimental sessions, if
that is possible.

Allan Kardec If your reason rejects what we consider irrefutable,
you must believe yourself to be intellectually supe-
rior to those who don't share your opinions. Far be it
from me to doubt your talent and believe I know
better than you. Grant then that I've been deceived,
and let's have no further discussion about it.

Visitor   But if you succeed in convincing me, antagonistic as
I am toward your ideas, your success would support
the cause you defend.

A. K.   I'm sorry, but I don't have the gift of performing miracles. Do you believe that one or two meetings
would be enough to convince you? That would be a
true miracle. I needed more than a year of research to
be convinced; I didn't arrive at my conclusions indis-
criminately. Besides, I don't conduct public meetings. It seems that you are misinformed about the
purpose of our meetings, since we don't conduct
experiments to satisfy anyone's curiosity.

Visitor   Don't you want to add converts?

A. K.   Why should we try to convert anyone? It's not my
                intention to force belief. When I meet people who sin-
                cerely want to inform themselves and who honor me
                by asking for explanations, I'm happy to answer them,
                within the limits of my knowledge. However, I don't
                try to change the minds or convictions of people. There
                are already a large number of people ready to consider
                a new belief. Why should we waste time with those
                who aren't interested?

                I'm certain that conviction will come to everyone
                sooner or later, and that unbelievers will be carried by
                the current. A few supporters, more or less, won't
                change the outcome. Therefore, I'm not planning to
                solicit people who aren't interested in learning about
                the Spiritist Doctrine.

Visitor   You might be more interested in converting me to
                your ideas than you think. Will you allow me to
                explain frankly and promise not to be offended by
                my words? These are my ideas about the subject, not
                about you. I am able to respect people without shar-
                ing their opinions.

A. K.   The Spiritist Doctrine has taught me not to take
                offense in differences of opinion. If your expressions
                are not accessible, I'll take them as insensitivity,
                nothing more. I am not easily disturbed by what
                others do or say. By this, you can judge one good
                effect of the Spiritist Doctrine.

                I told you that I have no intention of forcing anyone
                to share my views. I respect yours and I hope you'll
                respect mine. If you believe the basis of the Spiritist
                Doctrine a meaningless dream, you probably
                thought to yourself on your way here, "I'm going to
                see a lunatic." Please, feel free to express your
                thoughts freely; I won't take offense.

It's commonly said that Spiritists are a bit insane. If you think in that manner, I apologize for your having to endure a difficult situation today. Moreover, if you're certain that we won't succeed in convincing you, your visit will be fruitless—its only purpose will be to satisfy a personal curiosity.

Visitor   People can allow themselves to be deluded without becoming insane.

A. K.   You have indicated that you believe, as many do, that the Spiritist Doctrine is a fad that won't last. Yet, you must agree that an idea that within a few years has attracted millions of supporters worldwide, that counts among its followers educated women and men from all branches of knowledge, that is accepted avidly by well-informed individuals, is a singular phenomenon that deserves to be examined.

Visitor   Although I have my ideas, they aren't so absolutely firm that I wouldn't modify them in the face of convincing evidence to the contrary.

I told you that you would be interested in convincing me. I intend to publish a book expressing my opinion about a concept I believe to be untrue. Since the book would be critical of the Spiritist Doctrine, I would not publish it if I were convinced of the truth of these ideas.

A. K.   I would never think of depriving you of such an opportunity. I'm more than glad to assist you in your investigative effort, even if your final position turns out to be unfavorable. I hope the book has a large readership because it will serve to publicize the Spiritist Doctrine. Attention is always drawn toward the subject that is attacked. There are many people who want to know the pros and cons of an issue, and criticism often brings the truth to light, even for those who aren't looking for it. In this way, publicity often promotes the very idea it intended to destroy. The question of spirits is so interesting and so relevant that just bringing it out into the open is enough to generate the interest to examine it thoroughly.

Visitor   Then, in your view, criticism serves no purpose, and public opinion is meaningless?

A. K.   I don't consider personal criticism an expression of public opinion, but as an individual judgment that may well be mistaken. History is full of important works that were initially criticized, yet were later regarded as great masterpieces. If, however, something is truly bad, no praise can make it good. If the Spiritist Doctrine is false in its principles, it will fail by itself; if however, it is right, no criticism can make a lie of it. To our way of thinking, your book will be nothing more than a personal estimation, and public opinion will decide the validity of your ideas. If the public finds that you were mistaken, your book will go unsold and your ideas will be deemed irrelevant, just like those that rejected theories about blood circulation, vaccines, and so forth.

I assume, however, that you are going to treat the question thoroughly, that you are going to study it in all its facets, that you will try to see everything that can be seen, that you will read everything written about the subject, that you will analyze and compare the diverse opinions, that you will seek the best possible conditions for systematic observations, that you will dedicate sufficient time to it; in short, that you will disregard nothing to arrive at the truth. If you are serious, then you must do all this, because only one who has done it can speak knowledgeably on the subject.

What respect would you have for a person who, without having studied literature or painting, becomes a self-appointed art or literary critic? It is a basic assumption that the critic knows the subject in

depth; otherwise, their opinion has no value. To criticize a theory, it is necessary to replace it with
another theory. Critics can't limit criticisms to saying
that a thing is good or bad; their opinion must be
justified in a clear and logical argument using the
principles upon which the theory being criticized is
based. How could they do this without knowing
those principles? Without an understanding of engi-
neering, can one evaluate the qualities or defects of a
particular machine? No. And your evaluation of the
Spiritist thought is just such a situation. At each
step, you will be caught in a blatant mistake; those
who have studied the subject will see immediately
that you are uninformed. They will conclude either
that you are not a qualified investigator or that you
are acting in bad faith, and you will be shamed.

Visitor   It is precisely to avoid that danger that I have come
to request your permission to attend some experi-
mental séances.

A. K.   And you believe that this will be sufficient to enable
you to speak knowledgeably of the Spiritist philoso-
phy? How will you be able to judge those experiments or even understand them, when you haven't
studied the principles upon which they are based?
How would you appreciate the results of metallurgi-
cal tests, for example, without an in-depth knowledge of metallurgy? Your project is the same thing as
presenting yourself to one of the members of the
French National Observatory without having studied mathematics or astronomy, and saying, "Sir, I
wish to write a book about astronomy proving that
your theories are false. Since I don't know the rudi-
ments of astronomy, I would like to use your tele-
scope once or twice, which should be enough for me
to become as knowledgeable as you."

Remember, only by extension does criticism
become synonymous with condemnation. In its

proper use and according to its origin, it means the act of judging, discerning. Criticism can therefore be favorable or unfavorable. To critique a book is not necessarily to condemn it. A critic who undertakes the task should do it without preconceived ideas. However, the examination can't be impartial if, in the mind, the critic has condemned the book even before opening it.

Yet this has been the case of the majority who have spoken against the Spiritist Doctrine. They form an opinion merely upon hearing its name, acting like a judge who would pass sentence without trial proceedings to first examine evidence. The consequence would be an incorrect judgment, and instead of convincing, would cause laughter. A large number of those who have seriously studied the question have changed their minds about the Spiritist philosophy and phenomena, and more than one adversary has become a convert after discovering that the Spiritist Doctrine is very different from what they had supposed it to be.

Visitor   You are speaking of reading entire books. Do you think it's possible for journalists to read all the books passing through their hands, particularly those concerning new theories that they'd have to investigate and verify? That would be the same as expecting printers to read all publications coming off their presses.

A. K.   To such logic, I can only answer that when we lack time to do a thing conscientiously, it's better not to do it at all. It's preferable to produce only one good work, rather than ten bad ones.

Visitor   Please don't think that my opinion was formed frivolously. I've seen tables that turn and produce sounds like knocks. I've seen people write what they claim the spiritual beings dictate to them. I am, nevertheless, convinced that there is trickery in this.

A. K. How much did these people charge you to show you those things?

Visitor Nothing, of course.

A. K. Now, there you have very unusual con artists. Until now, altruistic con artists have never been found.

Let's suppose that a trickster wanted a little entertainment. Is it believable that everyone else in the party might have gone along with the sham? Why would they make themselves accomplices to a fraud? You might say that it's for the purpose of entertainment . . .

I agree that on one occasion they might participate in such play. Yet when the game lasts months and years, I believe the cheater is the victim. It's unlikely that anyone would spend hours sitting at a table, simply for the pleasure of promoting a false idea. The pleasure would not equal the bother.

Before judging this a fraud, it's necessary to ask what could be gained by the deception. And you must admit that there are people involved who wouldn't indulge in the slightest suspicious activity, people whose character already guarantees integrity. It would be quite different if it concerned a theatrical spectacle, because profit is a strong seduction, but even if a fraud were exposed, the deception would not in any way affect the reality of Spiritist principles. Just because poor quality wine is sold, one should not conclude that good wine doesn't exist. The Spiritist Doctrine is no more responsible for the acts of those who abuse its name or exploit its ideas, than the medical profession is for the actions of quacks or religion is for priests who misuse their ministry.

Because of its novelty and even because of its nature, the Spiritist Doctrine lends itself to abuses. However, it also provides the means by which to recognize the abuse. It rejects those who turn mediumship away from its higher purposes and use it to earn a living as an instrument of fortune-telling and frivolous readings. The Spiritist Doctrine outlines its own limits and defines what it can or cannot say or do, what is or is not within its competence, what it accepts and what it rejects. Therefore, only those who judge the Spiritist Doctrine on appearance or those who have met fakes calling themselves Spiritists to gain clients declare "This is Spiritism!"

Upon whom, ultimately, will the ridicule fall? Will it be upon the fakes who practice their trade? Will it fall upon the Spiritist Doctrine, whose statement of principles belies these fraudulent claims? Or, rather, will it fall upon the critics, who speak of what they don't know or knowingly alter the truth?

Those who tag the Spiritist Doctrine with practices that are contrary to its very essence do so either through lack of knowledge or malice. In the first case, there is negligence; in the second, bad faith. In the latter case, they become like those historians who, in the interest of supporting a political position or a theory, alter historical facts, but by these means, end up disgraced and the position they defend discredited. I don't expect that critics should necessarily agree with our ideas, even after having studied them. We will in no way oppose those who don't think as we do. What is evident to us may not be evident to others. People judge things from different points of view and, even from the plainest fact, people will draw their own conclusions.

If, for example, a painter paints a white horse on canvas and some say that white isn't effective, that black would be more appropriate—nothing wrong in that. It would be erroneous, though, to affirm that the white horse is black. This is what most of our adversaries do.

In summary, everyone is at complete liberty to praise
or censure the principles of the Spiritist Doctrine, to
deduce from them whatever good or bad conclusions they wish. Still, conscience imposes upon the
critic the obligation of saying what he or she knows
to be true, not the contrary. Well, the first condition
for that is that they shouldn't criticize what they
don't completely understand.

Visitor Let's return, please, to the rapping tables. Isn't it
possible for them to be rigged with some device?

A. K. It's constantly the same question of good faith.
When a fraud is exposed anywhere, I'll be first to
help make it public. If you uncover deceptive practices or discover fraudulent acts, I won't defend
them. The Spiritist Doctrine is the first to repudiate
them. Whoever exposes such abuses pays the
Spiritist Doctrine an important service. However, to
generalize those accusations, deserved only by some
isolated individuals by casting censure upon a large
number of honest people is an abuse of another
kind—it's slander.

Granting, as you believe, that the tables were rigged, it
would require an ingenious mechanism to produce
such varied movements and sounds. How is it possible that its inventor is still unknown? One would
expect that person to be quite famous since this mechanism is found all over the world. We must also agree
that this device is sufficiently delicate and subtle to
work anywhere on any table without revealing its
trickery. Why is it that since Tertullian,[3] who wrote
about turning and talking tables, until the present, no
one has seen or described such a device?

Visitor   Here you are mistaken. A celebrated surgeon recognized that certain individuals could contract a leg muscle to produce a cracking sound similar to that of knocking on a table. The surgeon concluded from this that mediums entertain themselves at the expense of their credulous customers.

A. K.   If it's a snap of the muscle, then it's not the table that is rigged. Each time someone uses this explanation, it's an acknowledgment that the true cause isn't known. I respect the knowledge of the wise surgeon, but I find that his theory presents certain flaws when used to explain the rapping tables. First, it's remarkable that this ability, exceptional up to now and seen as a pathological case, has become so common. Second, the medium must have a very strong wish to mystify, since that person must be willing to make the muscle snap for three consecutive hours without any personal gains except fatigue and pain. Third, I don't quite understand how the muscle can be called to account for the doors and walls on which knocks are heard. Fourth and finally, it's necessary to attribute quite a marvelous ability to that snapping muscle to enable it to move a heavy table, lift it, open it, close it, maintain it suspended in midair without any support, and finally, cause it to break into pieces upon falling. Certainly no one believes that a muscle could possess so many qualities. (*Revue Spirite*, June 1859, page 141, "Le Muscle Craqueur.")[4]

■■■

[3] *Translator's Note: Tertullian, Quintus Septimius Florens: (c 160-225 AD) Latin Church Father; lived in the ancient city of Carthage in what is now Tunisia; coined the word Trinity as one God manifested in three persons; developed understanding of original sin and relationship between faith and reason; influential writer and thinker of the early Christian Church. Tertullian appears to be one of the earliest persons on record to be familiar with talking tables, or "mensa divinatoriae," as they were called in antiquity.*

Has the renowned surgeon that you mention studied the phenomena of table rapping by examining the individuals who produced them? Has he studied these phenomena in all their phases? Has he verified that the muscular contraction was able to produce all these effects? No, he observed an abnormal physiological trait in some individuals who never concerned themselves with knocking tables. Seeing a surface parallel between that effect and those that the tables produce, he arrogantly concluded that all those who claim to make tables speak must have the ability to snap the short outer bone of the leg, and are nothing more than tricksters, whether they are princes or craftsmen, whether they receive payment or not.

Had he explored the phenomena, he would have seen the inadequacy of his theory. Instead, he decided to proclaim his "discovery" to the entire scientific community. Wasn't his hastiness rather compromising for a man of science? Who in the community today gives that pronouncement any consideration? I must confess that if I required surgery, I would certainly hesitate before confiding in that surgeon; I would fear that he might diagnose my illness with the same lack of insight.

You expected his opinion to support your crusade to crush the Spiritist Doctrine, but you see that it doesn't. I am perfectly capable of answering in a similar way to other arguments you may wish to raise, but I hope you'll make use of more reliable sources.

Visitor   Meanwhile, revolving tables are out of fashion today and no one bothers with them. Why did that happen, if it's such an important phenomenon?

■ ■ ■

⁴ *Translator's Note:* Revue Spirite—*journal published by the Société Spirite de Paris. The first issue came to light in January 1858. Allan Kardec was its founder and editor until his death in 1869. The Revue Spirite is currently owned by the Union Spirite Française et Francophone and published quarterly in partnership with the International Spiritist Council. For the online edition visit http://www.spiritist.org/larevuespirite.*

A. K.   Because from the table phenomena came something even more serious, a complete field of investigations, an ethical philosophy of the greatest interest to thoughtful people. When these people had nothing more to learn from tapping tables, they were no longer interested in them.

To fickle people, who don't want to examine anything thoroughly, that phenomenon was merely a pastime; an entertainment they abandoned once they were bored with it. Scientific inquiry cannot rely on such people. The period of curiosity was followed by one of systematic observation. The Spiritist Doctrine then became the domain of serious people, who didn't regard it as entertainment but as a means of self-instruction.

Still, people who consider it a serious matter don't dabble in experiments out of curiosity, and even less to satisfy those who have hostile thoughts. Since they aren't playing a game, they don't permit themselves to be used as playthings by others. I am one of these people.

Visitor   Nevertheless, only an experiment can convince anyone, even one who is motivated by curiosity in the beginning. If you work only with people who are already convinced, you preach to the converted.

A. K.   It's one thing to be convinced, and another to be open to accepting new ideas. It's to the latter group of people that I direct my attention; I'm not concerned with people who think it foolish to hear about what they call illusions. Those who have a sincere desire to gain knowledge are identified by their interest in investigating the phenomena seriously. They are not merely curious to attend a couple of experimental meetings. Belief must be built upon a series of methodical observations over a period of time.

Spiritist phenomena[5] differ from the physical sciences because they can't be reproduced at will; they must be studied when they happen. It is through a long, methodical observation and analysis that one discovers the proofs that escape the first glance, especially when one is either unfamiliar with the conditions required to produce the phenomena or has preconceived notions about them.

There are many proofs for the methodical and reflective observer, for whom an apparently insignificant word or fact constitutes a ray of light, a confirmation, while such facts have no meaning at all to anyone who observes them superficially or out of simple curiosity. For this reason, I don't conduct experiments without considering the element of probability.

Visitor   But everything must have a beginning. How can the person who knows nothing, who has seen nothing, but who wishes to learn, do so when you don't furnish them with the means?

A. K.   I make a great distinction between one who doesn't believe for lack of knowledge and one who is skeptical by dogma, i.e., who invariably shapes scientific inquiry to his convenience. When I meet people who have an honest interest to learn, I gladly spend time with them. However, there are people whose desire to learn is nothing but superficial curiosity.

■ ■ ■

[5] *Translator's Note: Spiritist phenomena refers to a broad range of paranormal phenomena obtained by mediums such as: clairvoyance, clairaudience, automatic writing, spirit rapping, transportation of physical objects (apports), levitation of the medium or of nearby objects, table turning, materialization, speaking in tongues, and so forth. Allan Kardec labels them as Spiritist solely to affirm the differences in the seriousness of purpose and method that distinguishes the Spiritist work from other venues of psychic work. Indeed, this category of phenomena is universal. There is nothing in them that may be characterized as exclusive to the Spiritist Doctrine. In addition, it is necessary to make clear that Allan Kardec employed the word 'mediumship' to characterize the mechanism of the whole class of phenomena. With the advance of knowledge, it became clear that certain phenomena are produced by the individual, i.e., the subject is not a medium or intermediary for the occurrence. Clairvoyance is an example of such phenomena.*

Instructing them is a waste of time because when they don't immediately find what they are searching for, and it might annoy them if they were to find it, the little that they see is insufficient to destroy their prejudices. So they misjudge the results obtained and ridicule the experiments. That's why it is not worthwhile to conduct experiments for them. To anyone who sincerely searches for knowledge, I would say:

You cannot take a course in experimental Spiritism as you would in physics or chemistry. Nobody is a master of producing phenomena at will, and the spirits often frustrate all our foresight. And because the phenomena are not necessarily orderly or interrelated, the experiment you come to witness may hardly fit your initial plan.

Start your learning with the theory; read and analyze the works of Spiritist research, for in them you will learn the underlying principles and the nature of the phenomena. The narratives of spontaneous cases and their explanations will lead you to understand the mechanisms of the phenomena. The theory and your study of the cases reported will strengthen your ability to overcome obstacles and will form the basis of your belief. Then, when you are presented with the opportunity to observe or participate in an experiment, you will understand it, no matter how the facts are presented, because you won't see anything extraordinary.

That is my advice to anyone who says they want to learn more. By their response, it's easy to recognize whether they are motivated by anything more than curiosity.

SECOND DIALOGUE

THE SKEPTIC

Visitor   I understand the value of the preliminary study of which you just spoke. As to my own position, I'll tell you that I'm neither in favor of Christian Spiritism nor against it. In fact, I must confess my ignorance of the doctrine, yet the subject greatly interests me. Among my acquaintances, there are both supporters and adversaries of it and I have heard very contradictory arguments on the topic. I would like to submit to you some of the objections raised that seem worth considering.

Allan Kardec I would be pleased to answer your questions, to the best of my ability. Spiritism is a field of study of recent origin and there's still much to be learned. It would be presumptuous on my part to pretend I can answer all your questions.

The Spiritist Doctrine is related to the fields of philosophy, metaphysics, psychology, ethics, and all the natural sciences; it's an immense field that can't be examined in just a few hours. Surely you understand that it would be physically impossible to repeat everything I've published about this subject. I suggest you do some reading in advance, because it will provide you with the answers to many questions that may come to mind. Furthermore, such reading will serve both to avoid repetitions and demonstrate your sincere interest in the subject.

Visitor   Agreed.

SPIRITISM AND SPIRITUALISM

Visitor   First, I must ask you about the need for creating new terms, such as Spiritist and Spiritism, as substitutes for the ordinary words spiritualist and spiritualism, which everyone understands. I have heard some classify such terms as barbarisms.

A. K.   For some time, the word *spiritualist* (as related to philosophical spiritualism) has enjoyed wide acceptance. The dictionary defines it as "one who tends to interpret things in a spiritual sense; one whose doctrine is opposed to materialism."[6]

All religions, from a philosophical perspective, are necessarily founded upon spiritualism. Anyone who believes that something exists within us beyond the material is a spiritualist; however, this doesn't imply a belief in the spirits and their manifestations. How would you be able to distinguish those who do have this belief? You'd be forced to specify each spiritualist as someone who either does or does not believe in the spirits. New concepts need new terms.

Look at it this way: If I had classified the *Revue* as spiritualistic, its character still would not have been

■ ■ ■

[6] *Translator's Note: The author's emphasis on the different meanings of spiritualism and Spiritism is particularly relevant for the French language, in which the book was originally written. In English, the distinction between these two words is less clear. For instance, according to the* Oxford English Dictionary *(O.E.D.), Spiritism and spiritualism are synonyms in the specific sense of indicating "the belief that the spirits of the dead can hold communication with the living, or make their presence known to them in some way, especially through a 'medium'; the system of doctrines or practices founded on this belief." Nonetheless, the O.E.D. does indicate a more general definition of spiritualism as the "... advocacy of a spiritual view or estimate of things, especially as a leading principle in philosophy or religion," which is more in line with the definition offered by Kardec. In order to facilitate the reader's understanding, the word 'philosophical' appears in parenthesis before spiritualism when appropriate. In addition, the word 'spiritualism,' as employed in this work, should not be confused with the religion known as Modern Spiritualism. While there are similarities between the Spiritist Doctrine and Modern Spiritualism, the differences are significant enough to justify a distinctive treatment.*

specified. Even with "spiritual" in the name, it still might say nothing about the spirits; in fact, it might even deny them. Some time ago, I read an article in a philosophy journal that the author said had been written from the spiritualist point of view. Believers in spirits would have been quite disappointed if, misled by that statement, they thought they would find some agreement between the points in the article and their own ideas.

The terms *Spiritist* and *Spiritism* were adopted because they express, unequivocally, the notion of spirits. While every Spiritist is necessarily a spiritualist, not all spiritualists are Spiritists. These terms and their distinctions would be useful even if the spirits were purely a fantasy, because erroneous concepts, like accurate ones, should be expressed in precise, proper terms. These words are no more barbarisms than those that the sciences, the arts, and industry are creating daily; for sure they are not more barbaric than those which Gall[7] imagined for his terminology of the mental faculties, such as: "secretiveness," "acquisitiveness," "destructiveness," and "amativeness."

You know that there are people with contentious natures who criticize and oppose anything they do not originate themselves. Those who provoke such squabbles only reveal their own narrow-mindedness. By seizing upon such trifles they show a lack of good sense.

The words spiritualism and spiritualist are British, but have been employed in the United States ever since spiritual manifestations first began to appear.

■ ■ ■

[7] *Translator's Note: Gall, Franz Joseph (1758–1828): German anatomist and physician who developed phrenology, a system for studying the skull, which, it was claimed at the time, revealed the intelligence and personality of an individual. He was the first scientist to identify the difference between gray and white matter in the brain and spinal cord.*

For a while, they were also used in France. However, when the terms Spiritist and Spiritism appeared, the public immediately accepted them as valuable distinctions.[8] Today their use is so widespread that the very adversaries who once called these terms barbarisms now use them. The sermons and pastorals that denounce Spiritism and Spiritists would create enormous confusion if they were directed toward spiritualism and spiritualists.[9]

Barbarism or not, those terms are commonly used in all European languages; they are the only terms used in all the publications, favorable or not, produced abroad. Just as chemistry once had to create a vocabulary to express special phenomena of that science, we have created special terms for our field of study. The words spiritualism and spiritualist are no longer employed by anyone except the followers of the American school.

DISSENTING EXPLANATIONS

Visitor   It seems to me that the disparity of ideas within what you call a science[10] is your downfall. If your science were based on facts, wouldn't it be the same in America as in Europe?

■ ■ ■

[8] *Translator's Note: This may have happened for a short period of time during the heyday of the phenomena, but the words spiritualism and spiritualists regained widespread acceptance after the 1870s. It must be noticed that they stand for ideas that are considerably different from Spiritism and Spiritist.*

■ ■ ■

[9] *Translator's Note: In a few particular situations in the text, the word 'Christian' was added as a qualifier for Spiritism. This was done when there was a beneficial value in characterizing the intrinsic personality of the movement. While the phenomena and research findings are value-neutral, the moral philosophy of the Doctrine is essentially Christian, as it rests wholly on the New Testament.*

■ ■ ■

[10] *Translator's Note: See Note 1 at the end of the Preface.*

A. K.   I will say that such a disparity only exists in form and doesn't affect the essence; it's limited to the way some positions are interpreted and doesn't constitute a radical schism in the principles, as some of our adversaries claim without having studied the question.

Yet, can you tell me of any science that, in its beginnings, didn't have disagreements until its principles were clearly established? Don't we still find disparities even in well-established sciences? Are the experts in any of these well-established sciences in perfect agreement on all its points? Don't experts have differences of opinion? Do the scientific conferences always present a picture of perfect and cordial understanding? In medicine, aren't there both the Paris School and the Montpellier School? Haven't major discoveries in other sciences also produced schisms between those who wanted to advance these discoveries and those who wanted to maintain the status quo?

Referring to Spiritism, wouldn't it be natural that when the mediumistic phenomena became more prevalent, before any theory was presented, each person had his or her own interpretation and looked at the facts differently? Where are those primitive interpretations today? They all faded before a more comprehensive explanation.

It only took a few years to establish the grand unity that prevails today. The few exceptions are those who became attached to the first conceptions and wouldn't change. What theory or religious philosophy offers a comparable example? Has the Spiritist Doctrine produced even a hundredth of the schisms that for so many centuries split the Church, and that still divide it today?

It's truly interesting to see the childishness to which the adversaries of the Spiritist Doctrine resort, which suggests that they lack any serious arguments; after all, if they did have serious arguments, they would use them. Their position is based on ridicule, negativity, and misrepresentations, but never on one single decisive argument. The fact that they haven't found a vulnerable point in the Spiritist Doctrine is an indication that its spreading is on a solid base. Less than ten years old, [in 1865] it already counts more followers than any other school of thought could claim after an entire century of existence.[11]

Mere criticism can't destroy the Spiritist Doctrine. To say about phenomena "this can't happen" or "that's an absurdity" isn't enough; it must be demonstrated categorically that the phenomena in question can't be produced and, in fact, haven't been produced. That is something nobody has done yet.

THE MATTER OF DECEPTION

Visitor   Can't the same phenomena be produced outside of Spiritist meetings? And from this, couldn't it be the case that they don't have the origin attributed to them by the Spiritists?

A. K.   Does the fact that something can be imitated mean that it doesn't exist? What would you say about the logic of someone who claims that all solid gold must be merely gold-plate just because gold-plate exists? All things have the potential of being imitated.

Some cheats once believed that, because of its popularity and the debates it engendered, the phenomena could be exploited. To attract crowds, they

■ ■ ■

[11] *Translator's Note: This book was first published in France in 1860, three years after the publication of The Spirits' Book in 1857. For all purposes, the publication of The Spirits' Book marks the birth of the Spiritist Doctrine.*

staged fake mediumistic phenomena—just as they had already staged performances with trance subjects.[12] All the rogues claimed, "This is Spiritism!" When bogus appearances of spirits were exposed as frauds, wasn't it proclaimed that Spiritism had been dealt a deathblow?

Before pronouncing such a final judgment, one ought first to recognize that the claims of a cheat aren't trustworthy, and second, to investigate the differences between a real fact and a simulation. For example, nobody buys a diamond without first making certain it's not a fake. Even a superficial investigation would have established that the conditions under which Spiritist phenomena take place are different from the charlatans' setups. Such a precaution would also show that *true Spiritists aren't concerned with making ghosts appear or telling people's fortunes.*

Only malice or bad faith could cause one to confuse the Spiritist Doctrine with magic and witchcraft, since the former stands completely against the practices, formulas, and cabbalistic words of the latter. Some adversaries even go so far as to compare Spiritist meetings to witches' Sabbath assemblies, where the strike of midnight is awaited so that ghosts may appear.

One day a friend of mine, a Spiritist, attended a performance of Shakespeare's Macbeth and was seated next to a newspaper journalist he didn't know. When the scene of the witches began, my friend heard his neighbor say: "Beautiful! We're going to attend a Spiritist meeting. It's just what I needed for my next article. Now I'm going to know exactly how

■ ■ ■

[12] *Translator's Note: In the French original, Allan Kardec utilized the words 'somnambulism', 'somnambulic', and 'somnambulist' in reference to the phenomena in which the medium goes into trance, or into a half-conscious state of mind.*

these things develop. If I were to meet one of those crazy nuts here, I would ask them if they recognize themselves in the scene they're watching."

"I am one of them," my Spiritist friend said to him, "and I can assure you that I see nothing that looks like a Spiritist service; I've attended hundreds of them and I've never encountered anything like this. If you've come here to collect information for your article, it won't shine for its truth."

Many critics don't have any solid foundations. And it is only they who will be ridiculed when their ignorance becomes known.

As for Christian Spiritism, far from being hurt by such attacks, its numbers have increased. That's because criticism has brought it to the attention of so many people who would not otherwise even have thought about it, and now, due to the public controversy, many recognize it as a serious concept to be examined and considered, and not as a pastime.

HELPLESSNESS OF ADVERSARIES

Visitor   I agree that among the critics of the Spiritist Doctrine there are many unscrupulous people, like those you just cited. On the other hand, aren't there worthy critics whose opinions have weight?

A. K.   I don't deny it. But to that I respond that the Spiritist Doctrine counts within its ranks many people of similar worth. In addition, the great majority of Spiritists are intelligent and well-educated people; only prejudice could lead one to say that its adherents are recruited from among the naive or uneducated. Consider this decisive fact: in spite of all the opposition of the learned and those with official power, no one has been able to stop the dissemination of the Spiritist Doctrine. Many among its opponents have had the intention of dealing the Spiritist Doctrine a mortal blow; however, in their attempts, they have all contributed to its popularity. Doesn't an idea that resists so many assaults, that advances in spite of the great criticism aimed at it, prove its strength and the soundness of its principles? Doesn't this phenomenon deserve the attention of thoughtful people?

Today, many agree that there must be some truth in such ideas, that perhaps it is one of those great, irresistible movements that stir up societies from time to time in order to transform them. This has always happened with revolutionary ideas. They inevitably encounter obstacles because they undermine the status quo—established interests, prejudices, and abuses. However, nothing can stop these new ideas; they are part of the Divine design for the progress of humanity. Their fast dissemination is validation of the truth they represent.

As I said before, the inability of adversaries to disprove the Spiritist Doctrine shows primarily that they lack sound arguments. They are amazed by the spread of the Doctrine, in spite of everything they do to derail it. They cannot find the cause for its growth because they search for it in the wrong place. Some attribute the growing number of cultured people who adhere to the Spiritist Doctrine as coming under the power of the devil, thus attributing to him strength greater than God's. Others attribute the wide acceptance of the Spiritist Doctrine to the increase in the number of borderline people, i.e., those suffering hallucinations. Their error is in believing that there is a single, primary source of Spiritist ideas and that they are the result of one man's creation. Consequently, they think that by refuting that one man's views, they can destroy the Spiritist Doctrine.

How can adversaries call Spiritist phenomena fakery, charlatanism, sleight of hand, or illusion, when thousands of individuals, independently, obtain such results? Is it plausible that they're all willingly fooling themselves?

The spiritual intelligences reveal themselves in all corners of the globe, contradicting the critics and confirming the principles of the Doctrine. The universality of spirit manifestation is a force that can't be explained by those who don't know the invisible world, just as those unfamiliar with the laws of electrical phenomena can't explain the speed with which a telegraphic message is transmitted and received. All denials lose their power against this force, much like the claims someone might make that the sun doesn't exist, although they can feel its warmth.

The progress of the Doctrine has not been checked because its principles are perceived as refreshing. Only by stopping the spirits from manifesting themselves could the opponents stand any chance of success. The reason Spiritists attach so little importance to the maneuvers of their adversaries is that they have experienced the facts themselves.

THE SUPERNATURAL EXPLANATION

Visitor   The Spiritist Doctrine tends to revive beliefs founded on the marvelous and the supernatural, demanding belief in superstition and popular myth, which seem to be totally condemned in this science-driven century.

A. K.   An idea is superstitious only when it has no basis in reality; but it ceases to be so when it is acknowledged as truth. The question is whether or not the spiritual intelligences manifest themselves; the Doctrine can't be dismissed as superstition until it's proven that spirits don't exist.

You say that your reason doesn't accept the explanation of spirit communication; however, those who do believe and who can hardly be called mad, are also guided by reason and much evidence. To which side should one be swayed? The great judge in this question is time—as it has been in all scientific matters that were once classified as absurd and impossible. You are actually prejudging in accordance with your personal opinion. We, however, judge only after having exhaustively observed and analyzed. Contrary to your preconceptions, the Doctrine seeks to destroy superstitious ideas, to demonstrate what is real and what is false in popular beliefs, and to denounce the absurdities borne of ignorance and prejudice.

I would go further and say that it is precisely the rationalism of our century that leads us to accept Spiritism. It is rationalism that makes it spread so quickly, rather than, as some mistakenly claim, a renewed fascination with the marvelous and the supernatural. The supernatural will disappear before the light of science, philosophy, and reason, just as the gods of paganism did before the brilliance of Christianity. "Supernatural" refers to everything that is above the laws of nature. Positivism[13] holds that nothing escapes the action of those laws, but have all these laws been identified? Throughout the ages, phenomena whose causes were unknown were regarded as supernatural.

The Spiritist Doctrine comes to reveal a new law by which communication with the soul of a departed person is a fact as natural as a telephone conversation between two individuals separated by hundreds of miles. The same is true of other Spiritist

■ ■ ■

[13] *Translator's Note: Positivism: A system of philosophy, originated by Auguste Comte (1798–1857), based solely on observable, scientific facts, and their relations to each other. It had a profound impact on the development of the sciences in the later parts of the Nineteenth Century and early decades of the Twentieth Century*

phenomena. Spiritism rejects miraculous effects that are above the laws of nature. It does not perform miracles, but rather, explains them in terms of natural laws. It, therefore, enlarges the domain of natural science, becoming a field of knowledge itself. However, these newly discovered laws carry ethical implications whose consequences also make Spiritism a philosophical system.

From this point of view, the Spiritist Doctrine corresponds to human beings' aspirations for the future. Its ideas about the future rest upon practical and rational bases that satisfy the positivist orientation of our century. You will realize this when you take the time to study it. (See also *The Mediums' Book*, Chapter II, and Revue Spirite, December 1861, page 393, and January 1862, page 21.)

THE OPPOSITION OF SCIENCE

Visitor   You said that you support your position with facts, yet you oppose the opinion of those scholars who dispute you or who explain the phenomena differently than you do. Why didn't they pay attention to the phenomenon of the revolving tables? If they had noted something serious, it seems to me, they wouldn't denigrate it; nevertheless, they're all against you. Aren't scholars the beacons of nations, and don't the former have the obligation to enlighten the latter? Why, when such a perfect occasion presented itself, didn't they reveal to the world the existence of a new force?

A. K.   You have outlined the duty of scholars admirably. It's a shame they have forgotten it in more than one case.

But before responding to your wise observation, I must correct a serious error in your saying that all learned persons are against us. As I mentioned earlier, it is precisely among educated people of all countries that the Spiritist Doctrine draws a large number of sympathizers. It already counts many learned minds of all nations among its large following. Judges, professors, artists, writers, officials, dignitaries, and ecclesiastics, recognized for their culture, have also embraced the Spiritist movement. Besides, intelligent people are not exclusively the product of universities.

Does Spiritism deserve to be condemned just because it hasn't acquired the sanctions of conventional science? If those in the natural sciences were never wrong, their opinion would carry greater weight, but unfortunately, experience proves that science has been wrong. Haven't scientists dismissed many discoveries that later brought glory to their discoverers? Wasn't it due to the opinion of elite scholars that France refrained from developing the steamship? When Fulton[14] came to Bologne to present his plan to Napoleon I, didn't the French Academy of Sciences decide, upon examining it, that it was unattainable? From this, should we conclude that the members of the Academy are unqualified and that the abuse they receive from certain tasteless people is justified? Certainly not. There's no one who doesn't recognize their eminent knowledge; still, they aren't infallible. Therefore, their pronouncements aren't indisputable, especially when concerning new ideas.

Visitor I grant that scholars are fallible, but by virtue of their knowledge, their opinion carries value. If they were on your side, they would lend great weight to your cause.

■ ■ ■

14 Translator's Note: Robert Fulton (1765–1815): engineer and inventor who developed the first useful submarine, the Nautilus, and torpedo (1800), and who produced the first viable steamboat, the Clermont (1808).

A. K.   However, nobody can be a good judge of something outside his or her competence. If you wanted to build a house, would you contact a musician? If you were sick, would you go to an architect? When you are involved in a lawsuit, do you consult a ballet dancer? No, each has an area of competence.

The physical sciences rest upon the properties of matter, which can be manipulated at will; their phenomena use material forces for agents. Spiritist phenomena have intelligent beings as agents who have independence and free will, who are not subject to our desires, and who, therefore, escape laboratory experimentation and calculations, remaining outside the domain of natural sciences.

Scientists deceived themselves when they attempted to experiment with spirit beings in the same way they experiment with electrical devices. They were unsuccessful, as well they should have been, because they presupposed an analogy that doesn't work. Then, without going any further, they concluded, by negation, that spirits don't exist. This was a hasty assumption and time is correcting it daily, as it has corrected many others. Those who so hastily dismissed the infinite power of the Creator will see their error exposed in time.

The traditional scientific research centers are not, and never will be, able to make a definitive pronouncement on this question. It is as far beyond their boundaries as the question of whether God exists. Asking them to evaluate Spiritist phenomena is foolish. The principles of the Spiritist Doctrine are a question of personal belief that doesn't depend upon scientific approval. The backing of some scientists has no power to create conviction. When positive public opinion about the Spiritist Doctrine has been established, the academics will finally accept it on the strength of the evidence.

Let this generation, with its prejudices and self-centeredness, pass and you'll see the same thing happening with the Spiritist Doctrine that happened with many other theories that were resisted at first but which would be ridiculous to question nowadays. Today, the believers in Spiritism are called crazy; tomorrow, it'll be the turn of its detractors. This is what happened to those who didn't believe the Earth rotated around the Sun. However, not all wise people made the same judgment—a wise person being anyone of knowledge who believes in thorough study, whether or not they have an official title. Many made the following rationalization: "There is no effect without a cause, and even ordinary effects can lead to solutions of the most difficult problems."

If Newton had not paid attention to the fall of an apple, if Galvani[15] had disbelieved his maid and called her a lunatic when she spoke to him about frogs that danced on a plate, perhaps we still wouldn't know the law of universal gravitation or the abundant properties of electrical energy. The phenomenon lightly referred to as the dance of the tables is no more ridiculous than the dance of the frogs. Perhaps a thorough study of the phenomena of the "dancing" tables (and the entire class of spiritual phenomena) will unlock secrets of nature that will revolutionize humanity's perspective of the world, when the proper key is turned.

Since so many people are concerned with Spiritist phenomena, and notable people have made them subjects of study, they must present some truth. A sham could not be so widespread. It might entertain certain circles, even a certain society, but it wouldn't

■ ■ ■

[15] Translator's Note: Luigi Galvani (1737–1798): Italian physician and physicist, best known for the discovery of electricity and for his experiments (with frogs) that established the presence of bioelectric forces in animal tissue.

spread around the world. Let's be wary of denying the possibility of what we don't understand; sooner or later, we may have to recant and that would severely discredit our judgment.

Visitor   Very well. Though I'm not a wise person, I think the same way as the wise person, reasoning with wisdom and prudence, who asks: "What is the foundation for the belief in the existence of spirits and, above all, their communications with us?"

A. K.   That belief is based upon facts and supported by reason. I, myself, did not adopt it until after a meticulous examination. Having acquired the tools of empirical investigation in my study of the natural sciences, I diligently probed this new field in its innermost particularities. I searched for explanations, as I'm not used to accepting any idea without knowing the how and the why of it.

Here is the reasoning of a wise doctor, formerly a skeptic and today a fervent supporter:

It is said that invisible beings can communicate with us. Why deny it? Before the microscope was invented, did anyone suspect the existence of millions of tiny little beings that cause so much devastation to the agricultural economy? Why is it physically impossible for there to be beings in space who escape our senses? Do we pretend to know everything?

If these invisible beings who surround us are intelligent, why can't they communicate with us? If they have a relationship with human beings, they must play a part in their destiny, in the happenings of their lives. Who knows—they may be one of the powers of nature, one of the hidden forces of which we're not aware? What new horizon might open to our reason? What a vast field for scientific observation! The discovery of the invisible world has greater significance than that of the infinitely small; it is more than a discovery, it is a revolution in ideas. How much light can this discovery shed? How many mysterious things can it explain? Believers are ridiculed, but so were all great discoveries in the beginning. After all, wasn't Christopher Columbus spurned, greeted with disdain, treated as stupid?

Some say these ideas are so strange that one shouldn't give them credit. Nevertheless, it has only been half a century since it's been possible to have instant communication between two points around the globe, to cross France in a few hours, to sail a ship against the wind with energy produced by boiling water, or to use water as a means of illuminating and warming ourselves. Half a century ago, the proposition that we could illuminate all of Paris by means of the energy generated in one reservoir of an invisible substance would have seemed preposterous. Therefore, is it so absurd for space to be peopled by intelligent beings who have left their material envelope after having lived on Earth? Doesn't such a possibility explain many beliefs that have persisted since remote times? These things definitely deserve an in-depth study.

These are the reflections of a wise, unpretentious physician. They are shared by many other enlightened men and women who have taken a hard look with an open mind at the phenomena. They studied it without forming opinions in advance and have had the modesty not to say, "We don't understand, so it can't be true." Rigorous observation and logic eventually led them to conviction. If those ideas had been an illusion, do you think that these prudent minds would have adopted them? Do you think they could have been victims of an illusion for so long?

The possibility of unseen beings populating space is certainly not absurd and, therefore, should be sufficient to demand more examination. After all, a short time ago, who would have thought that a single drop of limpid water could contain thousands of beings whose tiny size confounds the imagination?

Visitor   But we can't conclude that a thing exists just because it's hypothetically possible.

A. K.   Exactly, but you can't dispute that once an idea is accepted as possible, it has already advanced to the point where it is no longer absurd. It must then be verified by a methodical observation and analysis of facts. Both sacred and secular history proves the antiquity and the universality of belief in a Supreme Being and a future existence, beliefs that have been perpetuated throughout the ages and are found among even the primitive peoples.

The Spiritist Doctrine, then, is not a modern creation. Everything proves that the ancients knew it very well, perhaps better than we do. However, it was not taught, except with mysterious secrecy that made it inaccessible to the masses who were deliberately abandoned in the quagmire of magical beliefs.

The facts themselves fall into two categories: those that are spontaneous and those that are provoked. Among the former are the visions and appearances, the noises and movement of objects without a cause, and a great number of uncommon effects that we used to look upon as supernatural, but today seem simple to us because we don't accept the supernatural. The latter are those obtained through mediums.

FALSE EXPLANATIONS OF THE PHENOMENA

Visitor   Most criticism is directed primarily at the provoked phenomena. Let's put aside all supposition of charlatanism, and grant complete good faith. Isn't it possible that mediums are victims of hallucinations?

A. K.   I'm unaware that the mechanism of hallucination has been clearly explained. As it's now defined, hallucination is a most singular effect and worthy of study. It's a shame that those who wish to explain Spiritist phenomena in terms of hallucination can't define it first.

Several facts are not accounted for by the hallucination hypothesis, such as tables or other objects moving around, raising themselves, or knocking. A table moves about a room without anyone touching it, lifts from the floor, and remains suspended in space without any support, and finally falls back to the floor and smashes to pieces—all that can't be the effect of hallucination.

I agree that a medium could be led to see what doesn't exist. However, how is it possible that all those present simultaneously see the same vision? How, then, are similar "visions" occurring in other countries? If hallucination were the cause, it would be an even more extraordinary phenomenon.

Visitor Granting the reality of the phenomena of rapping tables, wouldn't it be more rational to attribute it to the action of some type of energy, such as magnetic energy?

A. K. That was first thought, and if all the phenomena were limited to those material effects, there is no doubt that this explanation would suffice. However, when those movements and raps gave proofs of intelligence, when it was recognized that they responded telepathically and independently, one could only draw the conclusion that, **if every effect has a cause, every intelligent effect must have an intelligent cause.** If one admits that the phenomena are produced by some sort of energy, why not admit that there must be an intelligent impulse behind it?

When you see a communication device producing signals that transmit thoughts, you understand that the device itself is not intelligent, but that it's activated by an intelligent being. The same process occurs with the tables to which we referred. Do they or don't they produce intelligent effects? This is the question.

Those who attack the phenomena have not carefully investigated, yet they have drawn hasty conclusions, biased by ideas that often are based on information obtained through incomplete observation data.

Visitor If there's an intelligent effect, it may be a result of the intelligence of the medium, of the examiner, or even of the attending people. After all, it's been said that the answers received were always already in someone else's thoughts.

A. K. That hypothesis is also an error based on incomplete observation. If they had taken the time to study the phenomena in all its phases, they would recognize the absolute independence of the manifesting intelligence.

How can this argument be reconciled with the fact that many of the answers received were far beyond the medium's intelligence and education, or were contrary to the medium's ideas, opinions, and wishes, or those of the attendants? How does it explain the ability of the mediums to write in a language they don't know, or to write in their own when they are illiterate? At first, the argument doesn't seem irrational, I agree, but it is disproved by facts so conclusive that they are impossible to doubt. However, if the argument was valid, the phenomena, rather than being simply explained, would be even more extraordinary because it would infer that thought could reflect upon a surface in the same way as light, sound, or heat! That would truly be a miraculous phenomenon, and certainly a subject for scientists to exercise their sagacity. Yet in a meeting of twenty people, it would be extremely difficult, if not impossible, to identify whose thoughts are being reflected.

It is curious to see how opponents will seek explanations a hundred times more extraordinary and complicated than the ones presented to them.

Visitor Isn't it possible that a medium in a semi-trance state might enjoy a kind of extra-sensorial capacity that brings a momentary amplification of his intellectual faculties? Why don't the contents of the messages given through mediums go beyond those obtained through hypnosis subjects?

A. K. Unfortunately, that argument is difficult to sustain. The medium is neither in trance nor asleep, but is completely conscious, acting and thinking like the others, without exhibiting anything extraordinary. Some effects may encourage that supposition, but one who studies all the facts will recognize that the medium is gifted with a specific faculty that shouldn't be confused with that of a person in hypnotic trance. The medium's autonomy of thought is demonstrated by an abundance of evidence.

Leaving aside the written communications, what hypnosis subject has ever made a thought come out of an inert object? Have any of them ever been able to produce visible or tangible apparitions? Could any of them cause a heavy object to suspend in the air without support?

Can it be a hypnotic phenomenon that a medium in my own home, in the presence of twenty witnesses, drew the portrait of a young girl he had never seen, a girl who had been dead for eighteen months? Yet the portrait was a true enough likeness that it was recognized by the girl's father, who was present at the meeting.

Similarly, can it be that a table answers questions posed to it (some even asked mentally rather than spoken)? If we admit that the medium is in a hypnotic trance, it is difficult to believe that the table is also in the same state.

It is said that mediums only speak about what is known. How, then, can one explain the following occurrence plus a hundred others of the same kind? One of my friends, a very good writing medium, asked a spirit if someone with whom he had lost touch fifteen years before, was still alive. "Yes, he still lives," was the spirit's reply. "He lives in Paris, street so and so, number so and so." My friend went to that address and found the person about whom he had inquired. Was that an illusion? How was his own thought able to suggest this reply since there was a strong possibility that the sought-after friend, being of advanced age, was no longer alive? If, in some cases, we see answers that match the inquirer's thoughts, would it be rational for us to assume that it is a general law? Hasty judgments are always dangerous since they can be contradicted by facts still to be observed.

Visitor   The skeptics want facts, but in most instances, they never receive them. If everyone witnessed proof, doubt would no longer exist. Why, then, have so many sincerely interested people succeeded in seeing nothing?

A. K.   The reason is simple. They want the phenomena to happen at their will. One can't give orders to spirits; it is necessary to await their will. It's not sufficient to say, "Show me proof, and I will believe." It is necessary to persevere and allow time for the phenomena to take place spontaneously. Trying to force the event won't help. The phenomenon one most wants to see may take a long time, but others may happen in the meantime. The sought-after phenomenon will happen when it is least expected. To attentive observers, the events will be numerous and corroborate themselves, but those who believe that touching the crank is enough to make the machine run, deceive themselves.

What does a naturalist do when beginning to study the habits of an animal? Does he or she command it to do a certain thing, so as to observe it at their will? No, because they know the animal won't obey them. They observe the spontaneous behavior of the animal and record it when it happens. Simple good sense dictates that one must proceed in the same way with the spirits, particularly since they are intelligent beings with independent will. Interest in knowledge, without preconceived opinion, is demanded of anyone who wishes to study Spiritist phenomena.

Of course, there are dogmatic skeptics who deny all evidence and aren't convinced by any phenomenon or argument. Even after having witnessed specific events, they still persist in explaining the facts in their own way, saying that what they saw proves nothing. Many would be upset if the evidence forced them to agree with our explanation because confessing that they had made an error would wound their ego. These people serve mostly to disturb meetings, and they leave without gaining anything themselves. Therefore, we ignore them. We don't want to waste our time with them— what can you say to someone who sees nothing but trickery and cheating everywhere? Nothing. It is better to leave such people alone.

In addition to these dogmatic skeptics, there are those who want to see things their own way, who have already formed an opinion, and have a full explanation of the events. They don't understand that the results they see may contradict their expectations, nor do they want to place themselves in the conditions necessary to obtain viable results.

Whoever, in good faith, wants to observe the phenomena, must have an objective mind and neutral attitude. One must observe each event with untiring patience. This necessity also reflects well on the followers of the Spiritist Doctrine, since it proves that they have not formed their convictions lightly. Do you have the time and necessary patience? No, and you'll say this is due to a lack of time. Since you aren't interested in devoting the necessary time, you would be better off to stop concerning yourself with this matter.

ABOUT THE SPIRITS' WILL TO CONVINCE

Visitor As the spirits must want to make converts, why don't they try to convince people whose opinion would be influential?

A. K. It's because they don't necessarily attach the importance we do to such people. That isn't very flattering to those people, I agree, but we don't have the right to impose our opinion upon the spirits. They have their own manner of judging things, which doesn't always agree with ours. They see, think, and act from a different perspective. While our view is limited by the narrow circle in which we live, they are able to embrace the whole, unencumbered by our restrictions. Time, which seems so long and slow to us, is just an instant to them. Distance is only a simple act of volition, and some details of extreme importance to us are nothing but trivial in their view. However, they attach great importance to things that have consequences that may escape our understanding. To understand them, it is necessary to raise ourselves above the material plane and put ourselves in their position. Study and systematic observation have shown that we must rise to their level; they will not descend to ours.

The spirits like attentive and conscientious students. Such persons can expect an abundance of knowledge from them. What puts them off is not doubt born of insufficient knowledge, but the foolishness of pretentious investigators who don't investigate seriously, who want to manipulate events and participants like puppets. In dealing with the spirit beings, these skeptics reveal a deep hostility. Therefore, the spirits care little about what they say or think, knowing their day of truth will come. It's for this reason that I say it's intellectual fairness rather than preconceived opinion that is required.

ORIGIN OF MODERN SPIRITIST IDEAS

Visitor   One issue I would like clarified is the starting point of modern Spiritist ideas. Are they the consequence of a spontaneous revelation from the spirits, or the result of preexisting belief in their existence? I believe this question is important because, in the latter case, it is possible that the imagination may have played a part.

A. K.   As you said, the question is important, because it is questionable logic to attribute observed phenomena to preconceived ideas. If Spiritism were, in fact, founded upon preconceived notions of the existence of spirits, one could legitimately doubt its veracity; if the principle were an illusion, its consequence would also be an illusion. However, the genesis did not occur that way. Note that your chronology is reversed—the spirits are the cause, not the effect. When an effect is observed, the cause can be investigated, but discovering a cause before its effect is not natural. The hypothesis of the existence of spirits couldn't have been formulated if the phenomena hadn't been observed first, to which the interference of invisible intelligences was a probable explanation.

Actually, it was not even in this manner that such a thought was born. A hypothesis incorporating spirits was not originally formulated to explain these phenomena; the first explanations were based on physical causes, e.g., electricity. The analytical approach treated it as a physical event and was far removed from any speculation involving spirit intervention. When we couldn't explain everything using that hypothesis, it was discarded and we had to consider the possibility of an unseen cause, i.e., spirits.

I speak now of modern Spiritist ideas, since the belief in spirits is as old as the world itself. This is how these ideas progressed: spontaneous phenomena were produced, such as strange noises, raps, movement of objects, and so forth, without apparent cause. Nothing up to this point suggested a search for causes outside magnetism or some other energy with still unknown properties. It didn't take long, however, to recognize in the noises and movements an intentional and intelligent character, which led us to the conclusion that, if every effect has a cause, *every intelligent effect must have an intelligent cause.* The objects themselves couldn't have intelligence. Could it be the reflection of a person or persons present?

This was the initial supposition, as I have already told you. However, continuing experimentation generated undeniable proof of the independence of the communicating intelligence. It did not belong either to the object or to anyone present. Who was it then? It responded, declaring that it belonged to the incorporeal beings called spirits.

The idea of spiritual individualities was not preexistent nor was it deduced later. In a word, it was not born of someone's imagination, but was given to us by the communicating entities themselves, and everything that we learned about them was taught to us by them. Once the existence of those individualities was revealed and the means of communication established, it was possible to maintain continued conversations and to obtain information about their nature, the conditions of their existence, and their role in the visible world. If we could question the beings of the microscopic world this way, how many curious things we would learn about them!

Let's suppose that before the discovery of America, a telegraph cable had been stretched across the Atlantic, and at its European end, intelligent signals had been heard. It would have been immediately concluded that there were intelligent beings at the other end who wished to communicate. We would have signaled them and they would have responded, leaving us with the certainty of their existence. It would then be possible to learn about their customs, practices, and mode of being, in spite of our never having seen them. This is what happened in our relations with the invisible world. The material manifestations were signs and means of information that opened the way to more regular and continued communication. As better means of communication became available, the spirits abandoned those primitive techniques, like a person with a speech impediment who, on recovering speech, no longer needs signals to communicate.

Who were the inhabitants of that spirit world? Were they beings completely separated from humanity? Were they good or bad? The resolution of such problems was entrusted to experience. Until a sufficient number of observations shed light on the subject, it was widely open to speculation. Some believed the spirits to be superior in everything, and others saw them only as demons. Their words and acts were the only means to set the good apart from the bad.

Let's suppose that among the hypothetically unknown inhabitants of America, of whom we just spoke, some had spoken with elevated ideas, while others were noted by their coarse language; one would have concluded immediately that among them there were good and bad characters. This is what happened with the spirits. By their acts and words, they were categorized as good or wicked, wise or slow. In our relations with them, we must use our common sense to set the good apart from the mean, the true from the false, just as we do with human beings.

Extensive observation enlightened us about their moral qualities, their nature, and their constitution. They, themselves, made it known that some were very happy and others very wretched; that they were not beings apart, of an exceptional nature, but rather the souls of those who had already lived on Earth, where they had left their bodies behind. Today, they dwell in a space that interacts with ours. By indisputable signs, they recognize each other as well as relatives, friends, and acquaintances from earthly lives. It's possible to follow them in all the phases of their existence and to relate their present-day situation to their existence and experiences on Earth. In short, it was learned that they are not abstract, immaterial beings, in the absolute sense of the word. They possess an envelope that we call the perispirit, made of a subtle energy, and a vaporous, diaphanous nature.[16] The perispirit is invisible in the normal state, but by a process of condensation or molecular redisposition, it may become visible and even tangible, explaining the phenomena of apparitions and of contact. The perispirit is the link between the spirit and the physical body. When the body dies, the spirit abandons it, but retains the perispirit. The process is similar to taking off an overcoat while continuing to wear an undergarment, or as peeling a fruit that retains the pulp. The semi-material envelope of the spirit serves as the

■ ■ ■

[16] *Translator's Note: From the Greek, Perí means surrounding. The perispirit is the subtle body of the spirit. It serves as interface between the spirit and the physical body. Equivalent to the concept of the spiritual body referred to by St. Paul (1 Cor. 15:44), Theosophy's astral body or etheric double. In popular language, the soul in a visible form—ghost. Some movie productions have offered amazingly powerful representations of the spiritual body, e.g.,* Ghost, Matrix, Star Wars, Flatliners, The Sixth Sense, *and* What Dreams May Come

means for producing different phenomena, enabling the spirit to reveal itself to us.

In a few words, this is the origin of Spiritist ideas. It should be clear now, and it will become even clearer when you decide to study it in depth, that everything in the Spiritist Doctrine is the result of unbiased observation and not the product of preconceived ideas.

MEANS OF COMMUNICATION

Visitor   As to the means of communication, can you explain how these invisible beings are able to converse with us?

A. K.   I would be glad to. However, I'll have to make it a brief explanation; the full analysis is long and elaborate, and is presented in detail in The Mediums' Book. Still, before you have a chance to study the issue further, the little I will tell you will be enough for you to understand the mechanism and will shed light on the experiments that you'll be able to attend.

The existence of the perispirit, also known as the spiritual body, is key to the explanation of many things, including the possibility of certain phenomena. As to the means, they are quite varied and depend as much on the nature of the spirits as on the unique dispositions of the people who serve as their intermediaries. The most common means, almost universal, is through intuition—the spirits suggest ideas and thoughts to the sensitive. This is an unsatisfactory means, though, when compared to others that offer more tangible effects. Some entities communicate "yes" or "no" through raps, or indicate letters that form words. The raps occur by the movement of an object, such as a table striking the floor, or they can be heard crackling inside an object without it being moved. That primitive method is slow and makes more advanced communication difficult. Later on, different writing methods emerged.

In the beginning, less often now, it was common to use a moveable object such as a board, a small basket, or a box—the nature and substance of the object were irrelevant—to which a pencil was attached with the point resting on a piece of paper. The medium placed his hands lightly on the object, and the pencil traced the characters. This object was nothing more than an extension to the hand, a kind of pencil holder. Later, it was realized that this object was just an added complication whose only merit was to demonstrate the independence of the medium, who could just as easily communicate while holding the pencil himself.

The spirits also communicate through other means: articulate sounds, which can be heard in the air or in the interior of the ear; through the medium's voice; by way of visual phenomena and drawings; through music; and by many other means that a more complete investigation can identify.

Different modes of communication require mediums with different predispositions. Thus, we have mediums of physical effects, who produce such phenomena as raps and the movement of objects, and others with gifts of hearing, speaking, seeing, painting, playing, and writing. Writing has become the most common faculty, because it's an efficient means of communication, and particularly valued for the possibility of being developed through practice.

I'll examine with you two of the methods of writing: automatic and intuitive. To understand them, it is necessary to know their mechanism of action. In automatic writing, the entity acts directly upon the medium's hand, giving it an impulse totally independent of the medium's will and compelling the hand to write. The medium is not aware of the subject. In intuitive writing, the spirit transmits its thoughts directly to the medium's mind who then, more or less consciously, writes down the message; the medium's role is exactly that of an interpreter who transmits a thought that is not their own, but which they must first comprehend. Sometimes in the intuitive case, the spirit's ideas may be confused with the medium's, but experience helps to differentiate between them.

Equally satisfactory communications are received through these two methods, but automatic writing provides more categorical evidence of the origin of the information. Generally, the quality of a medium is better appraised by the nature of the spiritual beings who assist him or her, and by the lofty content of the communications they receive, than by the means of execution.

Visitor   The process seems to be very simple. Would I be able to experience it?

A. K.   Certainly. If you are sensitive, you have the best means possible to convince yourself, since you cannot doubt your own good faith. However, I advise you not to attempt any experiment before careful study. Communications with the Beyond are complicated by more difficulties than one might think; they may bring inconvenience and risk for those who don't have the necessary experience, just as anyone, without understanding chemistry, runs the risk of burning their fingers if they attempt chemical experiments.

Visitor   Is there some way that one is able to recognize the possession of psychic aptitude?

A. K.   There is no known test for mediumship. Experimentation is the only means of learning if the faculty exists. There are many mediums and quite often they can be found among one's family members or close friends. Sex, age, and temperament don't matter; anyone can have the gift.

If mediumship were recognizable by an exterior sign, it would be a permanent characteristic. However, mediumship is essentially fleeting. Its physical quality is a product of combining the energies of both the spirit and the medium. Its reliability is a function of the spirit's willingness to engage in the exercise. So, we can conclude that spirits cannot communicate in the same way through all mediums. Conversely, a medium cannot assume permanent possession of the gift. Therefore, you should understand that you must undertake a long-term and methodical investigation if you want to learn the variations of the phenomena.

It's a mistake to believe that every spirit-being will come when called upon, or that it'll be able to communicate through the first medium available. For a spirit to communicate, conditions must be agreeable for it to do so, its situation must permit it to do so, and it must find the medium to be a suitable instrument.

In principle, we can communicate with spirits of all levels, including relatives and friends. However, they come at their own will according to their affinity towards those who call them, and not by the request of anyone who entreats them out of mere curiosity; if the spirit didn't care about the caller when on Earth, it won't care after death either.

Highly advanced spiritual beings take part in meetings with lofty purpose, where participants show introspection and have earnest objectives. They won't respond to trifling questioning or to experimentation.

Frivolous spirits go everywhere, but in high purpose gatherings, they keep quiet and remain withdrawn in order to listen, like students in a learned assembly. At frivolous meetings, they make fun of everything, often mocking the attendants and responding to everything without concern for the truth.

Spirit-beings apt to produce physical phenomena tend to be of a lower order. They are not necessarily bad natured, though. Higher-order spirits don't concern themselves with this order of activities. When such effects are needed, advanced spirits recruit the service of lower-ranking spirits, just as we avail ourselves of more physically strong workers to do heavy jobs.

SELF-SEEKING MEDIUMS

Visitor   Before undertaking extensive study, many people want to be sure they aren't going to waste their time. They want certainty, even if they pay a high price.

A. K.   Those who don't want to make the effort to study are motivated more by curiosity than a genuine desire to learn. The spirits have little appreciation for the light-minded. In addition, high spirits disapprove of greedy behavior. To think that virtuous beings, such as Fenelon, Bossuet, Pascal, and St. Augustine, would present themselves to the first caller at so much per hour is to have a false idea of our relations with the spiritual world. No, the communications from the Great Beyond are serious matters, not exhibits to be displayed.

We also know that Spiritist phenomena are not mechanical occurrences; they depend on the will of the spirit. Even if a person possesses a mediumistic aptitude, there's no guarantee that such person will receive a manifestation at any given moment.

Given that nonbelievers are inclined to doubt the good faith of mediums in general, their doubts would be increased if they were to encounter a profit motive. They would be justified in suspecting a paid medium of faking phenomena without the aid of spiritual entities, since the objective would be to earn money. Beyond the fact that absence of personal interest is the best guarantee of sincerity, the mere thought of calling upon the spirits of our beloved ones for financial profit is repugnant. Moreover, it's doubtful the spirits would go along with it. Only spirits of inferior classes, who have low ethical principles, would cooperate in such abuse. Furthermore, because these mediums are motivated by financial gain, they can't receive unreserved trust. The nature of the faculty does not allow it to be used as a means of income, because it depends upon a spirit's will. Moreover, it could suddenly disappear, which might cause the medium to fake it. However, even if the medium were acting entirely in good faith, it would be pure chance if, in a paid session, phenomena were produced that were exactly what had been requested as proof, since these phenomena can't be produced at will. Give 100,000 francs to a medium and he or she still won't succeed in compelling the spirits to do what they don't want to do. The gift would change the nature of intentions, as it would introduce a desire for financial gain where only the purest motivation existed. When one is convinced of this truth—that affection and affinity are the most potent means of assuring the spirits' presence—one will understand that requests from anyone motivated by financial gain is displeasing to them.

Just as faith can't be imposed, it's equally true that it can't be bought. Whoever needs facts to be convinced must demonstrate good intention through serious and patient study.

Visitor   I understand your logic, from an ethical point of view, but is it fair for those who use their time for the good of the cause not to be compensated for the time they divert from work that earns them a living?

A. K.   First of all, do they even do it in the interest of the cause, or is it for their own interest? If an individual left his or her employment, they did so because it didn't satisfy them, or because they hoped to earn more in another job, or to find one less tiring. There is no self-denial in doing something from which one hopes to derive profit. When a baker sells bread in the market place, is that an act of selflessness? Mediumship is not a trade. Mediums should look elsewhere for the means to earn a living.

Truly upright and devoted mediums, when they don't enjoy financial independence, seek ordinary means of support and don't abandon their professions. They only devote the time to mediumship that they can afford to without neglecting other activities. By devoting to spiritual activities part of the time normally allotted to entertainment and rest, they affirm their commitment to the highest purposes of life and become worthy of esteem and respect. Furthermore, the numerous mediums found within families eliminate the need for professional mediums, even if they could offer guarantees of success.

If it weren't for the discredit that accompanies professional mediumship, mercenary mediums would spring up everywhere and newspapers would constantly be full of their claims. For every legitimate medium, there'd be a hundred charlatans who, abusing or faking their ability, would do great harm to the Spiritist cause. Therefore, anyone who understands and takes to heart the dignity, true purpose, and best interest of the Doctrine would disapprove of any kind of financial motive in all that regards mediumship. Serious and sincere mediums—and I am referring to those who understand the sanctity of the mandate given to them by God—avoid even the slightest appearance that would lead to a suspicion of greed. They consider the accusation that they derive any profit from their faculty an insult.

You'll agree that a medium with this outlook would make a totally different impression on you than one you had to pay to see work, or even one who didn't ask for money, but whom you suspected of having ulterior motives. Wouldn't you naturally respect a person animated by a truly religious sentiment, stimulated by faith rather than the desire for personal gain? Although he or she might be a humble laborer, wouldn't they inspire more confidence simply because there would be no reason for you to doubt their sincerity? Well then, you'll find a thousand like them, and this is one of the factors that has contributed the most toward the credit and propagation of these ideas. If mediums had vested interests, the Spiritist Doctrine would not appeal to a quarter of the people who have embraced it today.

Paid mediums are extremely uncommon in Spiritist organizations in France because their gain-seeking motives would taint their reputation among the members of any group inspired by a true calling to service. Their business, furthermore, wouldn't be lucrative, not only because they would lose credibility, but also because they would have to compete with altruistic mediums who can be found everywhere. Because they may lack either the faculty or a sufficient number of clients, self-interested mediums often use cards, crystal balls, tea leaves, and so forth, hoping, in the absence of spirits' assistance, to attract people who still believe in such practices. If they discredited only themselves, the consequences of their deceit wouldn't be important. However, there are uninformed people who confuse mirages with real phenomena, and the profit seekers like to exploit this confusion by making them think that the imitation is really Spiritism.

You see, then, that since commercialization of paranormal gifts would have negative consequences for the Doctrine, we are right in strongly rejecting the use of compensated mediums.

Visitor All that is very logical, I agree, but altruistic mediums are not readily available and one feels hesitant to inconvenience them. That problem doesn't exist with someone who accepts payment, since we are not robbing them of their time. Many people who seek convincing evidence would find it much easier if public mediums existed.

A. K. If public mediums can't guarantee results, how can they lead anybody to conviction? Still, the difficulty you mention in finding available mediums is less crucial than the problems I've just indicated. People would see public mediums more as entertainers or fortune tellers than as sources of instruction. Anyone who wants convincing proof will find it with perseverance and good faith. Without these traits, no single experimental meeting will suffice to bring conviction, because when a person with a negative disposition attends a meeting, they tend to become more suspicious and may even abandon any further investigation, if no credible phenomenon takes place.

Apart from the ethical considerations, the development of Spiritist knowledge identifies the conditions in which manifestations are produced. It points out one major material difficulty in producing them: the need for affinity between the assisting spirit-being and the medium.

Let's forget, for a moment, any thoughts of fraud and trickery, and assume the complete honesty of the medium. For professional mediums to offer assurances to every client, their psychic faculties would have to be permanent and multi-faceted. They would have to be able to communicate with any spirit at any time, be constantly available to the public, and successfully make contact with the specific individualities requested. Yet this cannot be done by any medium, selfless or not. This possibility is out of their control.

We could go on and on with this conversation and turn it into a lesson on the Spiritist Doctrine. Let me stop by stressing that every mediumistic phenomenon rests on principles of affinity. Strong affinity between the medium and the spirit being is crucial. Without affinity, communications become unstable, unreliable, or plainly impossible. Very often, the affinity between the spirit and the medium is developed over time; rarely is it complete from the beginning. Thus, all mediumship is subject to natural laws. These laws represent an obstacle to the remunerated medium, since the possibility and the exactitude of the communications are factors under the control of neither the medium nor the spirit being.

Our rejection of the financial exploitation of mediumship is not without cause. The principles that govern our relationship with the invisible world are in opposition to the regularity and precision required by commitments to paying customers. The effort to satisfy paying clients may lead a medium to abuse his or her faculty. Don't conclude from what I have said, though, that all compensated mediums cheat people. I say only that the profit motive may impel them, consciously or unconsciously, toward inventing information, and this may make them suspect. As a rule, the medium's integrity is the only guarantee of genuine phenomena.

MEDIUMS AND SORCERERS[17]

Visitor   Since mediumship is nothing but a means of enter-

■ ■ ■

[17] Translator's Note: The term 'sorcerer', and the ensuing argument, must extend today to the whole class of individuals who use their gifts for selfish, harmful, or trivial purposes, or commercial exploitation. It includes palm readers, psychic readers, witchcrafters, stage mediums, etc.

ing into relations with invisible forces, aren't mediums and sorcerers more or less the same thing?

A. K. There have always been individuals who, by the
simple fact of producing unusual phenomena, were
labeled as sorcerers and accused of having pacts
with the devil. The same has happened to many
human beings who were extraordinarily knowledgeable. At times, some of those gifted individuals
abused and exploited public trust; hence, it is right
that they were maligned.

In most cases, it suffices to compare the moral fiber
of these so-called sorcerers to that of true and selfless mediums to see the remarkable differences
between them. However, most critics don't want to
make that effort. Far from reviving witchcraft, the
Spiritist Doctrine undermines it by showing that the
supposed supernatural powers attributed to its formulas, amulets, and talismans result from nothing
more than the manipulation of natural phenomena.
The similarity that some try to establish between
sorcerers and true and selfless mediums comes from
the erroneous belief that the spirits are at the service
of certain human beings. If they had studied the
Spiritist Doctrine before making these charges, they
would have known that it says that the *spirits are not
subject to anyone's whims; nobody can, at will, compel
them to respond to their call.* From this alone, we can
conclude that mediums are not sorcerers.

Visitor Then, all the results that certain celebrated mediums
obtain at will and in public is only quackery?

A. K. I did not say that at all. Such phenomena are not
impossible. Provided that a medium with the right
capability is available, certain spirits of a low order
may produce the phenomena. For them, it's just a
means of entertaining themselves. However, common sense rejects the idea that spirit beings come, no

matter how low their status, to play the clown and to do sleight-of-hand for the entertainment of the curious. Obtaining phenomena of that kind at will, and above all, in public, is always suspicious. In this case, mediumship and conjurer's tricks resemble each other so closely that it is often difficult to distinguish between them. However, before we draw any conclusions, we must observe carefully and consider both the character of the medium, background and accomplishments and the circumstances that the Spiritist Doctrine invites us to evaluate. For instance, feats performed by onstage psychics are theatrical by design and limited to a single kind of phenomenon. They are hardly capable of illuminating existential questions. The only sure guarantee of a medium's sincerity is the absence of financial interest in the phenomenon produced.

Whatever the degree of authenticity of public onstage phenomena, they serve to popularize the idea of spirit intervention. The controversy generated often stimulates people to look for additional information. These public displays certainly aren't the place to seek meaningful instructions about spiritual philosophy, but they attract the attention of the indifferent and force the more resistant to discuss the subject.

THE DIVERSITY OF SPIRITS

Visitor   I confess I don't understand the difference between serious and frivolous, good and bad spirits. It seems to me that on leaving the body, spirits are relieved of all traits and imperfections inherent in matter. Aren't they also immediately enlightened about all truths?

A. K.   Without a doubt, upon bodily death, spirits are freed of physical imperfections—that is, of pain and bodily infirmities. However, moral flaws are of the spirit, not of the body. Among the spirits, there are those who are more or less advanced in their moral and intellectual development. It would be incorrect to believe that spirits, once free from the physical body, immediately receive the enlightenment of truth. Do you believe that when you die, there will be no distinction between you and a brute person? If that is so, what's the use of your efforts to get education and improve yourself morally, when a barbarian, after death, will be as advanced as you are?

Spirits progress gradually and, sometimes, very slowly. Among them there are some who, because of their level of development, view things more accurately than when they were incarnated. Others, on the other hand, retain their passions, their prejudices and biases, until time and new trials help them to gain spiritual awareness. What I'm saying is the result of experience gathered from what the spirits tell us about their situations. It is, then, a basic principle of the Spiritist Doctrine that spirits exist at all levels of intelligence and ethical development.

Visitor Why aren't all spirit beings perfect? Why would God have created such diverse categories among them?

A. K. That's the same as asking why all the students of a college are not attending the same advanced philosophy course. All spirits have the same origin and the same destiny. The differences that separate them don't constitute differences in potential, but in levels of advancement. Spirits are the souls of human beings still distant from holiness. The physical and the spiritual worlds are in permanent interaction. The former returns inhabitants to the latter through deaths, and the latter replenishes the former through births. In each new existence, spirits take another step along the road to advancement, and when they acquire the total of knowledge and moral elevation available on our planet, they leave it to go to a higher world to continue their learning.

Spirit beings who form the invisible population of the Earth are, in some ways, a reflection of those living on it. They show the same vices and virtues. Found among them are the wise, the unaware, the liar, the prudent, and the frivolous, as well as philosophers, free-thinkers, and zealots. Since they don't get rid of their mindset and prejudices, all political and religious opinions are represented among them. Each one speaks according to his or her ideas, and what they say often merely reflects their personal opinions, which is why no one should believe blindly in what the spirits say.

Visitor That presents an enormous difficulty. In the case of conflicting opinions, how does one distinguish error from truth? I fail to see the usefulness of the spirits, or what we gain by conversing with them.

A. K. If they merely serve to give us proof of their existence and of being the souls of people, this alone would be of great importance to those who still doubt that they have a soul and who don't know what will become of them after death.

But we can learn much more from the spirits. However, like all philosophical endeavors, choosing between truth and falsehood and learning to dissect the deceptive suggestions of cunning entities, require long study and meticulous observation. Above the common mass of spirit beings, higher-order ones exist whose only purpose is to do good and whose mission is to guide humankind. It's good for us to know, appreciate, and understand them. They bring us crucial knowledge about ourselves and life. However, the study of the others is not without benefit. To know a group of beings well, it is necessary to study it in all its aspects. You, yourself, have proof of that; you thought that when spirits leave their bodies, they are divested of all their imperfections. Communication with them has taught us that this doesn't happen. They have revealed the true condition of the spiritual world, which greatly interests all of us, since we must go there someday.

As to errors that originate from differences of opinion among spirits, they disappear by themselves as one learns to distinguish the good from the bad, the wise from the unaware, the sincere from the hypocritical, just as we do among the living. Good sense will reject false ideas.

Visitor   My observation refers to scientific and other questions that we may submit to the spirits. Their divergent opinions about theories that are the subject of disagreement between learned men and women leave us uncertain. I understand that since they don't all possess the same level of knowledge, they can't know everything. What weight can we give, then, to the opinion of those who are more knowledgeable, when we are unable to distinguish between those who are right and those who are wrong? We might just as well address ourselves to people as to spirits.

A. K.   That observation indicates that you are still unaware of the Spiritist Doctrine's true nature. Whoever expects to find, in the Spiritist Doctrine, a shortcut to knowledge, an effortless means of discovering everything, is in error. The spirits are not messengers to bring us ready-made science. We would be quite comfortable if all we had to do is ask to receive knowledge, thereby escaping the need to study. Still, Providence wants us to work, to use our intelligence. Only by that effort will we acquire knowledge. The spirits aren't sent to free us of that duty. They are what they are and studying them is the purpose of the Spiritist Doctrine, so that by analogy, we may come to know what we will be one day. It's not their purpose to unveil what is supposed to be hidden, nor to reveal things before the appropriate time. Neither are the spirits fortune tellers. Whoever boasts of extracting certain secrets from them practices self-deception and becomes the sport of jesting spirits. In a word, the Spiritist Doctrine is a field of knowledge that utilizes scientific observation as methodology, not a game of fortune telling and speculation. We study it to learn about the condition of the spirits in the invisible world, the relationships that bond us to them, and their invisible effect on the physical world. We don't derive any material advantage from this investigation.

From this point of view, the study of any spirit being will always bring us something useful. Their imperfections, weaknesses, and even their ignorance are important elements of observation that help in establishing the nature of their world. When they don't instruct us directly, we educate ourselves by studying them, just as we do when we observe the customs of a people unknown to us. The enlightened spirits teach us many things directly, but always remain within the limits of our possibilities. We never ask from them what they are not at liberty to reveal. We are content with what they tell us. To go beyond that is to expose ourselves to the manifestations of frivolous spirits, who are always willing to talk about everything. Experience shows how far we can go with our inquiry.

PRACTICAL BENEFITS OF THE MANIFESTATIONS

Visitor Granting that all the evidence is legitimate and the Spiritist Doctrine is a reality, what is its practical benefit? Since we never missed it in its absence, it seems to me that we could continue to do without it.

A. K. We could say the same about railroads and steamships, without which we can live very well.

Humanity got along just fine before the discovery of new planets, before it was known that the Earth moved rather than the sun, and before the microscopic world and many other things were known. To grow wheat, a farmer doesn't need to know botany. Why, then, do learned people devote themselves to such studies? Is there anyone who would dare say that they waste their time?

If, to you, practical benefit means enjoying life, amassing a fortune, knowing the future, discovering oil wells or treasures, possessing an inheritance, or freedom from the effort of studying, then the Spiritist Doctrine is worthless. It can't affect the stock market or supply ready-made inventions to be exploited. From that point of view, the pure sciences would cease to exist! Many of them offer no practical advantage, commercially speaking.

However, everything that helps to lift a corner of the veil of ignorance advances the development of intelligence, widens the circle of ideas, and makes nature's laws more comprehensible. The spirit world exists as a consequence of those natural laws, and the Spiritist Doctrine helps to make it comprehensible to us. It explains the influence of the invisible on the visible world and their interrelationships, just as astronomy explains the relationship between the stars and the Earth. Spirits, thus, are seen as another agent of nature.

Even if its practical influence were limited to this, and its entire ethical system neglected, wouldn't the revelation of such a power already be of great importance? Would the revelation of an entirely new world be of no value when such knowledge directs us toward the solution of so many problems that were until now unsolvable, and when it initiates us into the mysteries that lie beyond the grave, a boundary that all of us, eventually, will have to cross?

However, the major strength of the Spiritist Doctrine lies in its moral influence. By bringing to light the existence of the soul, by proving its individuality and immortality, the Spiritist Doctrine strikes a blow against materialism, and it does so through the sheer force of empirical evidence rather than through theoretical arguments.

It's not appropriate to require more of the Spiritist Doctrine than it's able to give. One should not stray outside the limits of its providential purpose. Before serious progress was made in astronomy, people believed in astrology. Is it reasonable to say that astronomy serves no purpose because it no longer predicts the influence of the stars on our destiny? Thus, the Spiritist Doctrine is today for fortune-tellers and psychics what astronomy was to astrology, and what chemistry was to alchemy.

MENTAL DISEASE, OBSESSIVE THOUGHTS, AND SUICIDE

Visitor   Some people consider Spiritist ideas capable of disturbing one's mental faculties, and therefore, they speak against its dissemination.

A. K.   You must know the proverb, "Whoever wants a dog killed says that the dog is mad." It's not strange, therefore, that the enemies of the Spiritist Doctrine seize upon any and all pretexts to undermine it. This one is popular because it is effective in arousing fears and exploiting susceptible imaginations, although it doesn't withstand even the most superficial examination.

All major obsessions of the mind can cause insanity. The sciences, the arts, religion itself, furnish their share of obsessive personalities. Mental illnesses have roots in certain pathological states of the brain. If the instrument (the brain) has flaws, its faculties will be deficient. Insanity is, then, a consequent effect, the primary cause of which is an organic insufficiency that renders the brain essentially susceptible to defective judgments of reality. Therefore, some people rack their brains in various pursuits yet maintain a healthy mental life, while others, under the influence of the least mental excitation, become ill. When a predisposition exists, it takes on the characteristics of a fixed idea. An individual who is fixated on spirits might focus on them, just as he or she might focus on God, the angels, the devil, a treasure, power, parenthood, or a political or social ideology. It is quite likely that the religious fanatic would become an insane Spiritist, if spirits were his fixation.

An American tabloid supposedly reported that in one locality in America, it counted 4,000 cases of spiritual insanity. However, it's also known that our adversaries believe themselves to be the only ones gifted with reason. What a curious way of thinking! To them, we are all candidates for a mental institution, and, consequently, the 4,000 spiritualists of the locality in question were considered insane. What a joke! In the United States, there are hundreds of thousands of spiritualists (with whom we share interest in spirit communication and mediumship) and an even greater number in other countries of the world. The credibility the phenomena have gained, especially among the more educated, explains the widespread interest. The early entertainment character has disappeared. Much is made in France of the case of Victor Hennequin, but cynics forget that before he showed interest in spirits, Hennequin had already demonstrated the eccentricity of his ideas.[18]

■ ■ ■

[18] *Translator's Note: Victor Hennequin became known in Nineteenth Century France for his intense defense of Fourierism. Charles Fourier, a French social theorist, advocated the transformation of society into self-sufficient communities. This form of organization, Fourier claimed, was a more faithful representation of the Divine Order on earth. Victor Hennequin showed extremely radical behavior. Later in his life, he did develop interests in mediumistic communication. In his psychic experiments, he claimed to receive communications from "the soul of Earth" and to have received the Divine position of master of the planet.*

If turning tables hadn't appeared at that time (which, according to a witty pun of our adversaries, was what turned his head), his folly would have followed another path.

The Spiritist Doctrine doesn't have insane believers. I go still further and affirm that, if properly understood, the Spiritist Doctrine is a preventive medicine against some forms of mental problems and suicide. Among the most numerous causes of psychological problems, we must count disillusionment, disasters, and frustrated affections—elements that are also frequent causes of suicide. Nevertheless, the true Spiritist looks at matters of this world from such a higher point of view that these tribulations are no more to him or her than the small pitfalls of a long trek. Events that might produce violent reactions in others, affect them moderately. They know that life's adversities are trials that will contribute toward their advancement if they bear them with fortitude and without moaning, because their reward will be proportional to the courage with which they endured them. Their convictions give them a sense of acceptance that protects them from despair and, consequently, from one common cause of psychological problems and suicide. Beyond that, they know, through the accounts provided by spirits, of the deplorable destiny of those who voluntarily shorten their days, and this depiction serves to make them reflect. The number of those deterred from self-destructive intentions through the study of the Spiritist Doctrine is considerable. It's one of the great contributions of the Doctrine to humankind.

We must also include fear among the causes of insanity, primarily fear of the devil, which has deranged more than one mind. This fear has created a large number of victims by upsetting weak imaginations with petrifying pictures, which the clergy

takes pride in exaggerating. The devil, some ration-
alize, only causes fear in young minds; the notion is
therefore a useful restraint in disciplining them. Yes,
fear of the hobgoblin and the werewolf restrains
them for a time, but when they lose their fear, it
makes them harder to handle than before. Yet, many
people don't realize the detrimental effect that fear
may have on persons who have a fragile psyche.

Let's not confuse a pathological condition with the
problem caused by obsessive spirits. The latter does
not originate in any cerebral injury, but comes from
malevolent entities exerting influence on certain individuals, causing the appearance of mental disease.
This condition has always existed and is very frequently independent of any belief in the Spiritist
Doctrine. In such a case, common medication alone
may be useless. The Spiritist Doctrine not only
reveals the intrinsic causes of the disturbance, but
simultaneously offers the means to cure it by focusing
on the obsessive spirit. The Spiritist Doctrine offers
the remedy for, rather than causes of, the problem.

FORGETFULNESS OF THE PAST

Visitor   I am unable to explain to myself how humankind
profits from experiences acquired in previous existences when it does not remember them. Since we
lack these memories, each existence is as if it were
the first. In that sense, we're always beginning again.

Let's suppose that each day upon waking up, we
lost the memory of everything we did the day
before. Arriving at age seventy, we would be no
more advanced than we were at age ten. On the
other hand, remembering our misdeeds and the
consequences we endured would strengthen us to
behave better. Using your earlier comparison of a
human on Earth to a college student, I don't under-

stand how the student could profit from earlier learning if there was no retention of what was learned. Those discontinuities in the conscious life interrupt all relationships and make it, in a way, a new being. We may conclude then that our thoughts die with each of our mortal existences, which is akin to annihilation, since we'll be reborn without consciousness of who we were.

A. K.   From question to question, I will be led to give a complete review of the Spiritist Doctrine. All your arguments are natural and reasonable. My answers will be brief and in no way will they do justice to that which you can obtain only through serious study. Everything is linked together in the Spiritist Doctrine and when taken together as a whole, we see that its principles emanate one from another and mutually support each other. Once the Doctrine in its entirety is taken into account, what previously seemed contrary to God's justice and wisdom becomes natural and confirms that very justice and wisdom. This is the case with forgetfulness of the past, which cannot be suitably examined in separation from the rest.

If, in each one of its existences, a person's pasts are veiled, then nothing is lost of its acquisitions; it simply forgets how they were obtained. Still using the student analogy, it matters little to know where, how, and with which professors that student studied the subjects, as long as the lessons have been learned before moving to the next level. If discipline has made the student industrious and willing, does it matter when or how discipline was applied for being lazy and naughty? So, a person brings into each life, through intuition and innate ideas, the knowledge and moral virtues previously acquired. I include moral virtues because, if a person has been able to learn from experiences and improve in one life, he or she will uphold even stronger moral values in the next physical existence. Seasoned in the school of suffering and hard work, the person will be stronger. Far from having to begin all over, each possesses a background that continually grows and on which they draw for further development.

As for the second part of your argument, regarding annihilation, notice that forgetfulness only occurs during physical life. Once this ends, the spirit recovers its memory of the past. It can then judge the path it has followed and see what still remains to be done. So there is no discontinuity in spiritual life. Temporary forgetfulness is a blessing. At times, experience is acquired through rough trials and under grueling circumstances, the memories of which can be very painful and can increase the anxieties and tribulations of the present life. If life's suffering seems long, what would it be like if memories of the past were added to it?

You, for example, are a good man today, but, perhaps you owe that to the lessons you learned from your previous misdeeds. But those misdeeds might be repugnant to your conscience today. Would memory of having been hanged for a crime in another time be pleasing to you? Wouldn't you be distressed by the fact that your relations were aware of your crime? Does what you've done and suffered in a past life matter today when you are an esteemed man? In the eyes of the world, you are a new man, and in the eyes of God, a rehabilitated individual. Free from memories of a shameful past, you can fulfill your true potential. It is a new point of departure for you. Your previous debts are paid, and your duty is simply not to contract new ones.

Many people would like to be able to forget their youth years. Many, at the end of a life, have said, "If I had to do it again, I would not do what I did!" Well, then what they can't do in this life, they will do in another. Through intuition, their consciousness will bring the good resolutions they have made into a new existence. Thus, the progress of humanity gradually comes about.

Let's suppose, as is often the case, that a family member gave you many reasons to grieve in the past, perhaps ruining or dishonoring you in another existence. And that same individual, now a repentant soul, incarnated in your family for the purpose of redeeming himself through dedication and affection to you. Wouldn't it be mutually embarrassing if you both remembered your past animosities? Instead of being extinguished, the hate would be perpetuated.

The truth is that memories of the past would disturb social relations and be a hindrance to progress. Would you like proof of this? Take an individual who is sentenced to a jail term and who firmly resolves to become a good citizen. What happens when this person completes the sentence? Society, as so often happens, rejects him, and that rejection again induces the individual to crime. If, on the other hand, nobody knew about the person's past, he would be well received, and could walk with his head high, instead of being ashamed of past behavior.

According to the higher-order spirits, in worlds where good rules, the situation is different. There remembrance of the past is not painful. Inhabitants are able to remember previous existences, just as we recall today what we did yesterday. The remembrance of what they did in the past comes to them just like any other distant thought.

ELEMENTS OF CONVICTION

Visitor   I agree, my friend, that from the philosophical point of view, the Spiritist Doctrine is perfectly rational. Yet the question of the manifestations still remains, which can't be resolved except by empirical facts. It is their validity that many people contest, and you shouldn't find it surprising that they want to witness them.

A. K.   That is quite natural. However, as I want the demonstrations to be instructive, I would like to comment on the best conditions for one to observe and understand them. By observing them, a person will make the experience the most beneficial.

Logically, such a rational philosophy can't rest on illusory or problematic facts. The authenticity of the facts can only be guaranteed by a genuine cause. If one is real, the other can't be false. This is sensible, for fruits don't grow without a tree.

Not everyone has been able to witness the phenomena. The most obvious reason is because they didn't comply with the necessary conditions. They didn't have the patience and perseverance demanded. Nevertheless, this happens in all fields of scientific study: what some don't accomplish is accomplished by others. Every day we accept the results of astronomical calculations without making them ourselves. Be that as it may, if you find the philosophy good, you can accept it as you accept any other, maintaining your opinion about the ways and means that led to it or at least granting it as a hypothesis, pending a more ample investigation.

The elements of conviction are not the same for everybody. What convinces some produces no impression on others. This being so, a little of everything is required. It's a mistake to believe that physical experiments are the only means of persuasion.[19] I have noticed that, for some people, the most evidential phenomena didn't produce the least impression, while a simple written message conquered all doubts. When one sees a fact one doesn't understand, the more extraordinary it is, the more suspicion it arouses, and the more our thought tries to attribute it to an ordinary cause. However, if it's understood, it's soon acknowledged as rational, and its marvelous or supernatural character just vanishes.

Certainly the explanations I just gave you are far from complete, but brief as they are, I'm convinced they will cause you to reflect and, if circumstances permit you to witness some manifestations, you'll view them with less prejudice because you'll have a basis for your analysis.

There are two aspects to the Spiritist Doctrine: the experimental part of the manifestations, and the ethical philosophy. I am visited daily by people who may not have witnessed a phenomenon and yet believe as firmly as I do because of their study of the published works. For them, the phenomena are secondary and the central issue is the philosophy. They see it as so great and rational because they find in it the complete satisfaction of their inner aspirations, quite apart from the phenomena. They conclude that even if the manifestations did not exist, the doctrine would still resolve a multitude of supposedly unresolvable problems. So many people have told me that the begin-

■ ■ ■

[19] *Translator's Note: Theories that seek to explain spiritual phenomena can never be demonstrated by the experimental conditions that define the scientific method of physical sciences. The mediumistic phenomena involve the intentions, motivations, and values of more than one individual, in addition to the contributors from the spirit realm. The behavior of persons can seldom be predicted accurately, and much less, be controlled. This class of phenomena must be studied using nonexperimental techniques, such as observation and case studies. Investigations involving human behavior can only exceptionally satisfy the standards for truth of the physical sciences.*

nings of those ideas were already in their minds, albeit in a confused state. The Spiritist Doctrine coordinated them, gave them substance, and was like a ray of light! This is how many people explain the effect produced by reading *The Spirits' Book*.

Do you think there would be as many followers as there are today if we had never gone beyond the rapping tables?

Visitor   You are right in saying that a new philosophy had, in a way, its roots in the tapping tables. I didn't even suspect the consequences that came from something that was looked at as merely an object of curiosity. Now I see the vastness of the field opened by your method.

A. K.   You honor me by attributing that method to me when, in fact, it does not belong to me. It was deduced entirely from the teachings of the many illuminated spirit beings. I saw, I observed, I coordinated, and I tried to make comprehensible to others what I understood; this is the only part that belongs to me. There is a capital difference between the Spiritist Doctrine and other philosophical systems: the latter are works of enlightened men, while I can't claim the merit of having invented a single principle of the former, although you attribute that to me. We talk of the philosophy of Plato, of Descartes, of Leibnitz, but no one will ever say "the philosophy of Allan Kardec." I say this gladly, as a personal name has no value at all in a subject of such magnitude. The Spiritist Doctrine has architects (in the higher realms) of much greater importance, next to whom I am but a simple grain of sand.

SPIRITIST ASSOCIATION

Visitor   You have an association that is concerned with these studies.[20] Would it be possible for me to attend it?

A. K.   Not yet. While a degree in Spiritist studies is not required to be admitted, a minimum of knowledge is expected. As the meetings have a firm purpose and agenda, we prefer not to have the activities disturbed by elementary inquiries, or the presence of attendees hostile to the Spiritist ideas, since they might create unnecessary contention with their opinions. It's a scientific association that, like many others, is concerned with thoroughly examining different aspects of the Spiritist science and seeking new knowledge. It's a center where teachings collected from all over the world converge, and where questions regarding scientific development are elaborated and coordinated. However, it's not a school or an elementary course of studies. Later, when your convictions have been strengthened by study, your request for admission will be reevaluated. Meanwhile, you can attend one or two meetings as a visitor, as long as you maintain an attitude of respect and cooperation. You'll find there a gathering of serious and cultured people, the majority of whom are recommended because of their knowledge and intellectual standing. Visitors are treated with courtesy and are expected to behave accordingly. The meetings are not open to the general public. The society doesn't sponsor demonstrations for the purpose of satisfying curiosity, and it discourages the presence of entertainment seekers. It is for these reasons that our invitations are selective.

■ ■ ■

[20] Translator's Note: Société Spirite de Paris, France. See "Reflections by Allan Kardec" at the end of this book.

PROHIBITION OF PRACTICE

Visitor   I have one last question: Since the Spiritist Doctrine
has powerful enemies, couldn't they forbid its prac-
tice and associations and, in so doing, impede its
propagation?

A. K.   That would only serve to defeat their purpose, since
violence is the argument of those who lack good
sense. If the facts are false, the Spiritist Doctrine will
fall by itself. If they attack it, they do so because they
fear it, and only that which is real should cause concern. If, on the contrary, the phenomena are true,
then they are part of nature, and no one can revoke
natural laws with the stroke of a pen.

If Spiritist manifestations were the privilege of one
person, there's no doubt that eliminating that person would put an end to the manifestations.
Unfortunately for adversaries, they're not a mystery—nothing is secret and everything takes place
openly. The capacity to produce manifestations is
available to the entire world and they can occur just
as well in a palace as in a hut.

Adversaries can forbid the public practice, but it's
well known that the phenomena usually take place
in private. Since anyone can be a medium, who can
forbid a family in its home, an individual in the
silence of his room, or a prisoner in his cell, from
communicating with the spirit realm? It could even
be practiced in the presence of the police without
their being aware of it. Even if a government was
strong enough to deter people from working in their
homes, would it succeed in stopping such action in
neighboring countries and throughout the world?
Mediums can be found in every country.

The source of the Spiritist Doctrine is not among
human beings. It is the work of the spirits, who can't be
burned or imprisoned. The Spiritist ideas are a matter

of personal belief, rather than of allegiance to an organization. If Spiritist books were destroyed, the spirits would dictate others.

In sum, the Doctrine is, today, a consummate fact. It has already gained its place in public opinion and among modern philosophy schools. Although they are at liberty to reject it, those who disagree with it must accept its existence.

THIRD DIALOGUE

THE PRIEST

Priest   Will you allow me, sir, to ask you some questions?

Allan Kardec With pleasure, Reverend. Before answering them, I think it would be appropriate to say that I will do so with the purpose of informing you, without intention to proselytize. If you wish to understand this realm of ideas in more depth, you will find explanations in several books.

The Spiritist Doctrine's purpose is to combat incredulity and its disastrous consequences, by supplying proof of the soul's existence and of the afterlife. It addresses itself to those who don't believe in anything or who doubt everything and, as you well know, there are many such people. On the other hand, those who have religious faith, and find satisfaction in that faith, have no need of the Spiritist Doctrine. To anyone who says, "I believe in the authority of the Church and I adhere to its teachings without, in any way, searching beyond its tenets," the Doctrine replies that it doesn't impose itself on any person, nor does it coerce belief. Freedom of conscience is the result of freedom of thought, one of man's attributes. If the Spiritist Doctrine did not respect this freedom, it would contradict its own principles of tolerance.

From the viewpoint of the Spiritist Doctrine, any creed that keeps people from doing wrong to their neighbors is respectable, even if it's flawed in other ways. If someone were to believe, for example, that the sun revolves around the Earth, we would tell him, "Believe it if you want to, since it won't change the roles of these two celestial bodies; however, just as we don't violate your principles, we ask that you also respect ours." However, if a belief, innocent in and of itself, is transformed into an instrument of persecution and abuse, it must be opposed.

This is the conduct I have followed with representatives of various religions who have come to see me. When they asked about certain points of the Spiritist Doctrine, I made the necessary explanations, but I refrained from discussing their beliefs and interpretations. All human beings are free to evaluate religious dogmas for themselves. I have never approached anyone with the purpose of shaking his or her faith. Whoever seeks us as a friend is welcomed as such; those who disagree with us, we leave in peace. That is the advice I've always given to Spiritists, because I don't agree with those who assume the mission of proselytizing converts from other faiths. I have always told them, "Sow in the field of the unbelievers, where there is a harvest to reap."

The Spiritist Doctrine doesn't impose itself because, as I told you, it respects freedom of conscience. It also recognizes that all imposed faith has shallow roots. Its principles are open to scrutiny so each person may form his own opinion. Those who accept its principles do so freely and because they find them rational. At the same time, however, we bear no ill will toward those who disagree with our view. If there's animosity from the Church, we didn't provoke it.

Priest   If the Church sees a new belief system arise that contains principles it must, in conscience, condemn, can you argue its right to discuss and combat those principles in order to warn its faithful of what it considers a threat?

A. K.   In no way can we contest that right, which we also claim for ourselves. If that right had been exercised within the boundaries of polite debate, nothing would have been better. But if you read most of the material written by members of the Church and published in the name of religion—as well as listen to the sermons that have been preached—you will find them overflowing with injury and libel. The principles we defend are always badly misrepresented.

From the pulpit, we Spiritists have been called enemies of society and public order. We have been denounced and rejected by the Church, which suggests that it is better to believe in nothing than to believe in the soul according to Spiritist knowledge! If it were possible today, our detractors would stir up the fires of the Inquisition against us. In some places, Spiritists were censured to the point of being persecuted and injured on the streets, while the faithful were forbidden to hire Spiritists and were warned to avoid them as they would the plague. Women were advised to separate from their husbands, and husbands from their wives, in the campaign against Spiritism. Charity has been refused to the needy and workers have lost their livelihoods, just because they were Spiritists. Blind people have even been discharged, against their will, from some hospitals because they would not renounce their beliefs.

Tell me, Reverend, is that an honest discussion? Still, did the Spiritists retaliate against injury with injury, evil with evil? No! They've always faced everything calmly and in moderation. Public conscience, at least, recognizes that they weren't the aggressors.

Priest   Every sensible man deplores those excesses, but the Church can't be held responsible for the abuses committed by some of its unenlightened members.

A. K.   I agree. Yet should princes of the Church be classified as unenlightened? Read the pastoral letter of the Bishop of Algiers and others. Wasn't it a bishop who ordered the Edict of Barcelona?[21] If the Church tolerates shameful sermons from the pulpit, if it allows the publication of injurious and defamatory writings against an entire class of citizens, and does not oppose the persecutions exercised in the name of religion, it must approve of them.

In truth, the Church systematically rejected the Spiritists and tried to silence their voices. The nature and violence of its attacks compounded the original dispute and threw the Spiritist Doctrine into a new light. The Doctrine began merely as a philosophy; it was the Church who gave it greater scope and presented it as a formidable enemy—it was the Church, after all, that proclaimed the Spiritist Doctrine as a new religion.

Priest   A while ago, you advocated freedom of thought and conscience, declaring that every sincere belief is respectable. Materialism is a view like any other—why do you, as the church deny it the freedom you concede to all the others?[22]

A. K.   Certainly one is free to believe in whatever one wishes, or even to believe in nothing at all. We wouldn't bother a believer in any religion. In combating materialism, we do not attack individuals,

■ ■ ■

[21] *Translator's Note: Edict of Barcelona: By order of the Catholic Church, Spiritist books were confiscated and publicly burned in 1861.*

■ ■ ■

[22] *Translator's Note: In the French original the interlocutor in this single segment was identified as 'Free Thinker.' Considering that this personality doesn't appear anywhere else in the text, and that the flow of arguments is logical and internally consistent through the whole section, the translation team opted for treating "Free Thinker" as a typographical error. By respecting the structure of dialogue between the priest and Allan Kardec, the integrity of the chapter is maintained.*

but a philosophy. This philosophy, while apparently inoffensive, when rooted in the individual consciousness could become a moral ulcer.

The materialistic belief that everything ends at death, that all liability ceases with the extinction of bodily life, causes one to see the sacrifice of present well-being for the benefit of another as foolish. From such an attitude arises the belief that each person should look out for his own interests during earthly life, because with its termination everything ends. In brief, there is no reason to practice charity, fraternity, and morality because they have no basis. Why bother ourselves, restrain ourselves, and limit our pursuit of enjoyment today, when tomorrow we will be nothing? The denial of the future, the simple doubt about an afterlife, is the primary source of egoism, the origin of humanity's greatest evils. One must possess great virtue not to follow the current of immorality and social exploitation without any restraint other than one's own willpower. Reverence for human life can be a restraint for the average person, but it may not be so for the person who considers human life just a fortuitous and temporary biological event.

A belief in the afterlife, though, demonstrates the perpetuity of relationships, thereby establishing an interdependence and accountability that doesn't end with death. Acceptance of such a belief changes the course of one's ideas. If the afterlife were a simple myth, belief in it would be short-lived. The afterlife is an objective fact confirmed through reliable research evidence, and the Spiritist Doctrine has a duty, in the interest of human progress, to propagate this fact and demonstrate it to those who hold contrary belief. The Doctrine is accepted because it supplies proof, and because humans would much rather believe in a hopeful afterlife that compensates for the miseries of this world than believe in nothingness as the end. The prospect of being annihilated, of losing children and loved ones without hope for reunion, comforts very few people, trust me. That is the reason attacks against the Spiritist Doctrine fail to produce the least disturbance.

Priest   Religion teaches all those things, and until now, it was sufficient. Why is a new system of belief necessary today?

A. K.   If religion teaches enough, why are there so many disbelievers, religiously speaking? Religion does teach us, that's true. It commands us to believe, but many people cannot base their belief on blind faith. For them, the Spiritist Doctrine demonstrates what religion teaches in theory. Where does this proof come from? It comes from the manifestation of spirits. Furthermore, the spirits communicate with God's permission; therefore, if God, The Merciful, sends them to help abolish disbelief, it's irreverent to reject them.

Priest   Still, you can't contest that the Spiritist principles are in conflict with religion on several points.

A. K.   Oh! My Lord, Reverend, all religions will say as much: Protestants, Jews, Muslims, as well as Catholics. If the Spiritist Doctrine denied that a man's soul is individual, immortal, and subject to future suffering or reward; if it taught that one should live only for oneself; it would not only contradict all other religions of the world, it would also repudiate all moral laws—the foundation of human societies.

Far from that, the enlightened spirits proclaim that there is only one God, Who is sovereignly just and good. They also say that human beings are free and responsible for their own acts and that they are rewarded or corrected according to the good or wrong they have done. The spirits place above all else, the evangelical virtue of love (charity) and the sublime rule taught by Christ: to do unto others, as you would have them do unto you. Are these not the foundations of religion? They do more: they initiate us in the mysteries of the future life, which for us is not an abstraction anymore, but a reality, since it is those we knew who come to depict their situation, to tell us how and why they suffer or are happy. What's so antireligious about that? This certainty about the future, about meeting again those we loved, isn't that a consolation? The splendor of the spiritual life, compared to the petty worries of earthly life—doesn't that elevate our souls and strengthen us in the practice of good?

Priest   I agree that, in general, the Spiritist Doctrine is in accordance with the great truths of Christianity. However, can the same be said about the Christian dogma? Doesn't the Spiritist Doctrine contradict some of the tenets that the Church holds so high?

A. K.   The Spiritist Doctrine is, before everything else, a field of knowledge illuminated by scientific principles. It does not ponder points of dogma. As with other fields of knowledge, it has significant moral ramifications. As for how beneficial this knowledge is, you must only consider the ethical purposes discussed above.

Some people are greatly surprised to discover such a strong ethical angle in the Spiritist phenomena. This is a very important point and merits some development. Let's begin by making a comparison. Electricity, a force of nature, always existed and always produced the effects we observe today, plus many others that we still don't understand. Unaware of its true cause, people of an earlier time explained those effects in an extravagant manner. The eventual explanation of electricity's principles and the harnessing of electrical power destroyed a handful of absurd theories and shed light upon more than one mystery of nature. Back to the issue at hand, what electrical research and the physical sciences did for certain phenomena, the Spiritist Doctrine has done for others of a different order.

The Spiritist thought is founded upon the existence of an invisible world formed by incorporeal beings who populate space and who are the very souls of those who once lived on Earth upon which they left their material bodies. They are the beings we call spirits, beings who surround us and constantly exercise a great influence upon us, without our awareness of it. They take an active part in the mental world, and, to a certain extent, in the physical world. They are a part of nature. One can say, from a figurative perspective, that they are a power of nature, though not in the same manner as electricity or gravitation. The phenomena elicited from the invisible world have always been produced, evidenced by the fact that the histories of all peoples mention them. Only due to ignorance, could humans have attributed these phenomena to essentially nonintelligent causes.

The Spiritist Doctrine has shed light upon a great many questions, which until now were unanswerable or to which the answers were poorly understood. Its true character is more a field of knowledge than of a religion. The proof of this is that among its adherents are people from all beliefs who, as Spiritists, did not renounce their religious convictions. Strong Catholics, Protestants, Jews, Muslims, and even Buddhists and Brahmanists have been attracted to the Doctrine while continuing to perform all the duties of their religions—providing their clergy did not rebuff them. They are able to do so because the Spiritist Doctrine rests upon principles free from dogma. Its moral implications are, in every sense, those of Christianity because, of all belief systems, Christianity is the purest and most enlightened. Of all the religious believers of the world, Christians are the most apt to understand the Spiritist Doctrine in its true essence. Should Spiritism be condemned for that? Anyone can create a personal religion upon their own beliefs. Some may even build a new denomination upon their interpretation of certain religious principles. But it's a very great distance from that to the establishment of a new religion.

Priest   Nevertheless, aren't the spirits' presence requested according to a religious formula?

A. K.   True, religious sentiment dominates our meetings, but we don't have formulas. When we pray, the thought is everything, the formula is nothing. We invite spiritual assistance in the name of God, because we believe in God and know that nothing happens in the world without God's permission; therefore, the spirits won't come unless God permits it. We proceed in our work calmly and with reverence, a necessary condition for effectively observing the phenomena. We also know that respect is due to those who no longer live on Earth, whatever their condition in the spiritual world may be—happy or unhappy. And, we appeal to the good spirits, because we recognize that there are both good and bad ones, and we don't want the latter to have any influence on the communications we receive.

What does all this prove? Only that we aren't atheists, although we don't profess a traditional form of religion.

Priest   Well, then, what do the higher spirits say regarding religion? The good spirits ought to advise and guide us. Let's suppose that I didn't have any religion and wished to choose one. If I were to ask them to advise me about whether I should be Catholic, Protestant, Anglican, Quaker, Jewish, Muslim, or Mormon, what would their reply be?

A. K. There are two points to consider in evaluating religions: the general principles common to all, and the specific principles governing each of them. The former includes those principles about which we have been speaking, which all the spirits laud, irrespective of their stages of development. Ordinary spirits, without being malicious, may have preferences or opinions regarding specific principles. They may approve of this or that practice on the basis of personal conviction, earthly ideas, or for the sake of prudence, in order not to frighten pious consciences. Do you think, for example, that an enlightened spirit, addressing himself to a Muslim, would say anything critical of the prophet Muhammad, or suggest that only by converting to Christianity will the Muslim be saved from Hell? Of course not, because it would be insensitive and only cause a negative reaction.

Enlightened spirits do not generally concern themselves with such questions. Rather, they limit themselves to simply saying, "God is good and just. God desires only good." In other words, the best of all religions is one that teaches only what is in accordance with the goodness and justice of God; presents the greatest and most sublime idea of God; doesn't attribute to God the weaknesses and passions of humanity; helps human beings to be good and virtuous and teaches them to love one another like brothers and sisters; condemns every wrong done to a neighbor; doesn't condone injustice under any pretext; teaches nothing contrary to the unchangeable laws of nature; is led by ministers who set the best example of goodness, charity, and moral behavior; combats best and flatters least the pride and vanity of people; and, finally, one in whose name the least harm is committed. A good religion cannot serve as justification to any evil whatsoever. It must not leave any door open to wrong, either directly or through interpretation. Look, judge, and choose!

Priest   Nonetheless, certain points of Catholic teachings are
                 disputed by spirits you consider superior. Suppose
                 that those principles are indeed erroneous. Would
                 belief in them, according to these spirits, prejudice
                 the salvation of those who, right or wrong, consider
                 them articles of faith and practice them accordingly?

A. K.   Certainly not—as long as these principles encourage
                 such believers toward the practice of good, rather
                 than divert them from it. Even the most sincere belief
                 will hurt them, however, if it provides the occasion to
                 do wrong, discourages charity to a fellow human
                 being, or makes them harsh and egoistic—then they
                 don't act according to the laws of God, Who judges
                 thoughts before actions. Who would dare say other-
                 wise? Do you think, for example, that faith can jus-
                 tify a person who claims belief in God and yet
                 behaves in an inhuman or uncharitable manner?
                 Wouldn't those who have greater knowledge be
                 more culpable for such actions?

Priest   So, the fervent Catholic, who scrupulously fulfills the
                 duties of his religion, is not censured by the spirits?

A. K.   No, not as long as his conscience compels him to do
                 so—if he does it sincerely. However, if he is hypocriti-
                 cal, if he only pretends to be pious, then yes, he is
                 deserving of censure.

                 Superior spirits, those whose mission is to look after
                 humanity's progress, are against all abuses that
                 might retard this progress in any shape or form, no
                 matter their nature and the individuals or classes of
                 society that might benefit from them. It cannot be
                 denied that religion has not always been exempt of
                 abuses. Although there are many ministers who
                 carry out their duties with true Christian devotion
                 and who present Christianity as grand, beautiful,
                 and respectable, you must agree that many of them
                 haven't understood the sanctity of their ministries.

The spirits have no greater adversaries than those who defend such abuses—abuses that promote the idea that one religion should be replaced with a better one. If a particular religion is endangered, the blame should fall upon those who misrepresent it, who transform it into an arena of human passions, and exploit it to gratify their selfish ambitions.

Priest   You said that the Spiritist Doctrine does not debate dogmas. Nevertheless, it supports certain ideas condemned by the Church, such as reincarnation and the appearance of man on Earth before Adam. It also denies eternal punishment, the existence of demons, purgatory, and hellfire.

A. K.   Those ideas have long been debated. It was not the Spiritist Doctrine that started the controversy; these concepts are disputed even among theologians. Only the future can reveal the truth of such matters. Still, a grand principle dominates all: the practice of good, which is the superior law, the sine qua non of our future, as proven by the state of the spirits who communicate with us.

Believe in the flames and tortures, if you wish, as long as your belief impedes the practice of harmful deeds. However, your faith won't make these things real if they don't exist. You believe that we have one corporeal existence, but your belief won't prevent spirits from being reborn here or in some other place, if it must be, despite your wish to the contrary. You believe the world was created in six days of twenty-four hours each but, in spite of that, the Earth itself presents contradictory proof in its geological layers. You are convinced that Joshua made the sun stop, which doesn't change the fact that it's the Earth that rotates. You say that the date of mankind's first appearance on Earth was not more than 6,000 years ago. This doesn't prevent the facts from contradicting this idea, though. And what will be the reply when geologists prove, through obvious vestiges, that mankind's ancestors predate that period, just as they have already proven so many other things?

Believe, then, in anything you wish—even in the existence of the devil—if such a belief will make you a better person and more charitable toward your fellow man. The Spiritist Doctrine, as an ethical philosophy, recommends only one thing: the necessity of doing good and avoiding doing wrong. It is a science of observation that, I repeat, has ethical consequences that confirm and prove those great religious principles. As far as other secondary points, it leaves them at the discretion of each.

Note well, Reverend, that some of the points you spoke of are not, in principle, contested by the Spiritist Doctrine. If you had read everything we've written on this subject, you would have seen that the Spiritist Doctrine limits itself to giving such religious controversies a more logical and rational interpretation than the one commonly provided by the Church. The Spiritist Doctrine does not, for example, deny purgatory; rather, it demonstrates the necessity for, and justice of, the concept of purgatory. The Church has described hell as an immense furnace, but is it understood that way by higher theology? Evidently not. Theologians contend that this is simply imagery, that the fire is imaginary, a symbol for greater suffering. And, if it were possible to know the intimate thoughts of all humanity—even the most religious—who can reason and understand the eternity of punishment, you would find that the majority believe that the idea of an eternity of suffering is a denial of the infinite mercy of God.

Here's what the Spiritist Doctrine says in this regard: *The duration of punishment is subordinate to the rehabilitation of the guilty spirit. No predetermined amount of*

*time is pronounced for punishment of the spirit. What the
Law requires in order to terminate the spirit's suffering is
repentance and reparation—in short, a serious and effective improvement, a sincere return to good. The spirit,
thus, controls its own destiny. Its obstinacy in wrongdoing prolongs its suffering; likewise, its efforts to do good,
lessen or abbreviate its suffering. With the length of suffering dependent upon a change of attitude, the guilty spirit
that doesn't repent and never improves, suffers, so to say,
forever. For that consciousness, then, there is an eternity of
punishment. This suffering must be understood in the relative sense and not in the absolute. A condition inherent to
the inferiority of certain spirits is that they can't see an
end to their situation and believe they must suffer forever.
But when their souls open to repentance, God permits
them to glimpse a ray of hope.*

Certainly this principle conforms more to the justice of
God than the Church's dogma of eternal punishment.
According to this view, Providence disciplines while
the guilty one persists in wrongdoing, and bestows
grace when the guilty one returns to the path of good.
Who could have imagined that theory? Could we
have been the ones? No. The spirits teach it and give
evidence supporting it through the examples they
provide to us daily. The spirits, then, don't deny
future punishment; in fact, they come to describe their
own suffering. This portrayal is more convincing than
the thought of perpetual flames, because everything
in it is perfectly logical. The spirits' examples make it
plainly clear that this situation is a natural consequence of things. Even the inquisitive philosopher is
better able to accept it, because nothing in it contradicts reason. This is why Spiritist beliefs have guided
many people toward good, even materialists, upon
whom the fear of hell made no impression.

Priest   Doesn't the average person need more impression-
able images rather than a philosophy she or he is
unable to understand?

A. K.   That error has driven more than one person toward materialism, or at least, has driven many away from religion. The time has come when those images are no longer believable, and people who are unable to accept that one point, reject everything. They say: "If they presented a concept that is false as an unquestionable truth, then who can be sure that anything else they say is true?" If, on the contrary, a concept is demonstrated in a logical and rational way, then faith is strengthened. Religion gains by recognizing the progress of ideas. It runs into danger when it remains stationary while human beings strive to progress. Anyone who hopes to lead human beings today by exploiting fear of the devil and eternal torment is making a colossal error.

Priest   The Church, in effect, recognizes today that the traditional description of hell is a symbol, but that doesn't preclude the existence of devils. Without them, how do we explain the influence of evil, which cannot come from God?

A. K.   The Spiritist Doctrine doesn't recognize devils as such. However, it does acknowledge bad spirits whose behavior resembles that of so-called devils who cause wrongdoing by inciting wickedness. The difference between these wrongdoing spirits and devils is that the Spiritist Doctrine doesn't say that these are special beings created for, and devoted perpetually to, wrongdoing, or that they are an outcast species of creation and tormentors of the human race. Rather, they are still unevolved beings to whom God always gives another chance to repent and grow. In this, Spiritism agrees with the Greek Orthodox Church, which encourages its followers to pray for the conversion of Satan, an allusion to the improvement of wicked spirits. Note well, incidentally, that the word demon did not originally imply the idea of an evil spirit. Modern usage has given it

that meaning. Actually, the Greek word daemon sig-
nifies genius or intelligence. Still, today it is used to
mean only a cruel spirit.

Now, to recognize communications from evil spirits
is, in principle, to acknowledge the reality of all
manifestations. The question is really whether bad
spirits are the only ones that communicate, which is
what the Church says in order to support its sanc-
tion against communications with the spirit realm.

At this point, let's invoke reason and the facts. If the
spirits—good or bad—communicate, it can only be
with God's permission. Is it possible that God only
permits the wicked to communicate? Would God
give complete liberty to the wicked to deceive
humankind and prevent the good from serving as a
counterbalance against the schemes of the malicious
ones? To believe this would be to doubt God's goodness and to raise Satan to the stature of divinity. The
Bible, the Gospel, and Church fathers recognized the
possibility of communicating with the invisible
world, and the good are not excluded from that
world. Why, then, do we exclude them today? The
Church, by accepting communications from the
saints and the authenticity of certain apparitions,
negates the idea that we're only able to enter into
relationships with wrongdoing spirits. Assuredly,
when the messages received contain only good
things, when they instruct us in the most pure and
sublime evangelical morality—self-denial and love of
neighbor—or when they combat all aspects of evil, is
it logical to believe they come from the devil?

Priest   The Gospel teaches that the angel of darkness, or
Satan, transforms himself into an angel of light in
order to seduce people.

A. K.   Satan, according to the Spiritist Doctrine and the
opinion of many Christian philosophers, is not a real

being. He is merely the personification of evil, just as Saturn was once the personification of time. The Church limits itself to the literal meaning of the figure. It is a question of opinion I will not discuss.

Let's grant for a moment that Satan is a real being. The Church, by exaggerating his power to intimidate its followers, obtains exactly the opposite result—that is, the elimination not only of the fear, but also of the belief in such a personage, in accordance with the proverb, "Whoever desires to prove too much, proves nothing." The Church's methods represent him as eminently subtle, cunning, and crafty, but the Spiritist Doctrine shows that he's either a lunatic or a fool.

Once it's known that his purpose is to supply hell with victims and snatch souls from the power of God, it's understood that he directs his efforts against those who are good in order to induce them to wrongdoing. Consequently, he must transform himself into angel of light (according to the most beautiful allegory)—that is, he hypocritically simulates virtue. In so doing, he allows those who are already in his power to escape his snares. That's what we can't comprehend. Those who don't believe in God or the soul, who despise prayer and live immersed in vice, are his. Nothing remains but to bury them in the mire. Now, to incite *them* to return to God, to pray, to submit themselves to the will of the Creator, to encourage them to renounce the path of iniquity, to reveal to them the happiness of the chosen and the misery that awaits the wicked, would be the act of a fool. It would be more stupid than setting caged birds free with the idea of catching them again later.

Every sensible person is offended by the contradiction in the notion that only demons communicate. No one can believe that spirits are Satan's auxiliaries who try to persuade those who have denied God to return to God, or to encourage those who practice wrong to do good, or that they would console the afflicted, give strength and courage to the weak and, by the sublimity of their teachings, elevate our souls above material life. Therefore, who can believe that any relationship with the invisible world must be forbidden?

Priest If the Church forbids communication from the spirits of the dead, it's because it violates the teachings of religion, having been formally condemned by the Gospel and by Moses. It was Moses who pronounced the punishment of death[23] for those who participated in such practices, proof of how reprehensible these practices are in the eyes of God.

A. K. I beg your pardon, but you're mistaken. Such a prohibition is not found in any part of the Gospel; it is found only in the Mosaic Law. Therefore, it's a question of whether the Church places the Mosaic Law above the Gospel. That certainly would seem to be the case, if it were more Jewish than Christian.

■ ■ ■

[23] *Translator's Note: Deuteronomy 18:10 "Let no one be found among you who sacrifices his son or daughter in the fire, who practices divination or sorcery, interprets omens, engages in witchcraft, or casts spells, or who is a medium or spiritist or who consults the dead." Nowadays, Christian Spiritists are often confronted with the same arguments by other Christians. However, anyone who invokes such accusations should remember that, first of all, according to the Oxford English Dictionary, the word Spiritist only appeared in the English language in 1856 (Bible translators may have taken excessive license) Second, in the same source God is "supposedly" commanding Moses to kill the innocent women and children of the Heshbonites (Deuteronomy 2:35). If the truth of the latter is hard to accept, why shouldn't the same be said for the former. Further, the prohibition of Moses was made absolutely irrelevant by Paul later on as he considered, and regularly accepted advice from, the spirit realm. In Acts 21:4 he is warned through the mediumship of the disciples in Tyre "...through the Spirit they urged Paul not to go on to Jerusalem." Even though Paul considered such recommendation, he decided not to accept it and resolutely continued on his way to Jerusalem. Nobody in a sane mind could defend that the "Spirit" is the Holy Spirit because if it were, Paul would not dare to ignore the warning. The advice had to have come from a well-meaning spiritual friend who was associated with the practices of the local church.*

We must point out that, of all religions, it is Judaism that least opposes the Spiritist Doctrine, against which it doesn't invoke the Law of Moses, as do the Christian denominations. If the biblical prescriptions are the code of the Christian faith, why does the Catholic Church forbid the reading of the Bible?[24] What would they say if a citizen were forbidden to study his country's code of law?

Moses' prohibition regarding mediums was justified at the time because the Hebrew lawgiver wanted his people to break with all the customs brought from Egypt, among which was the practice we are discussing. In the days when Moses prohibited communication with the invisible world, the dead were not invoked to show respect and affection, to pay honor, or to express a sentiment of piety. They were invoked as a means of divination, as shameful tools of superstition exploited by charlatans. Under such conditions, Moses was right to forbid it. He pronounced a severe punishment against this abuse because rigorous measures were needed to constrain his undisciplined people. However, the sentence of death was too extravagant a condemnation on his part.

It's a mistake to cite the severity of punishment as proof of the level of culpability for invoking the dead. If the interdiction came from God directly, as the Church claims, it must also be God who ordained the punishment of death against the offenders. Since this punishment has the same sacred source as the prohibition itself, why doesn't the Church maintain it? After all, every Law of Moses is promulgated in the name of, and by the

■ ■ ■

[24] Translator's Note: Historical records indicate that until the mid part of the Nineteenth Century, the Church maintained strict regulations on the reading and interpretation of scripture. The rule was promulgated by the Council of Trent (1545–1564).

order of, God. If the Church believes that God is the author of the Mosaic Law and its punishments, why does it no longer observe them? If the Law of Moses is an article of faith to the Church on one point, why should it cease to be so on all others? Why does the Church refer to it when it needs to and reject it when it is inconvenient? Why doesn't it follow all its pre-scriptions—that of circumcision, for instance—to which Jesus submitted and which he didn't abolish?

There were two parts to the Mosaic law: first, the law of God as summarized in the tablets of Sinai, a law that was kept because it is Divine and which was fur-ther developed by Christ. Second, there were the civil or disciplinary laws appropriate to the customs of the time, which Christ virtually overlooked. Today, cir-cumstances are different, and that prohibition of Moses has no justification. If the Church forbids call-ing upon the spirits, can it prevent their coming with-out being called? Every day, we see manifestations of all kinds among people who were never concerned with Spiritist ideas. Many of them took place even before the Doctrine was made known.

Moses' action points, by the way, to still another contradiction in the Church's attitude toward the Spiritist Doctrine. The fact that he prohibited the seeking of contact with the spirits of the dead is in itself proof that they were able to respond; other-wise, it would have been a meaningless prohibition. If, in his time, spirits could make contact with men and women, they still can today and, if they are spir-its of the dead, they are not exclusively demons. Above all else, we must be logical.

Priest   The Church doesn't deny that good spirits can com-municate, since it recognizes that the saints have also manifested themselves. However, it doesn't consider as good those beings who come to contra-dict unchangeable principles of the Church. The

higher spirits teach that there are future punishments and rewards, true, but of a different kind
from those the Church teaches. The Church alone
can evaluate what the spirits preach and, consequently, distinguish the good lessons from the bad.

A. K.   This is the key question. Galileo was accused of
heresy and of being inspired by the devil because, in
revealing a law of nature, he disproved a belief that
was thought to be beyond attack. If the spirits had
endorsed all Church principles, if they had not promoted freedom of conscience or reproved certain
ecclesiastical practices, they would have been welcomed rather than classified as demons. All religious groups who believe themselves to be in exclusive possession of the absolute truth, consider any
system as flawed that is not entirely mainstream
with their point of view. The spirits don't come to
destroy religion but, like Galileo, they come to
reveal to us still undiscovered laws of nature. If
some articles of faith suffer because of this, it's
because, like the old belief that the sun revolves
around the Earth, those articles contradict the natural laws. The question, then, is whether an article of
faith can take precedence over a natural law. Once
that law is recognized, isn't it more rational to adapt
the dogma accordingly, rather than attribute the
new knowledge to the devil?

Priest   I know that the question of demons is interpreted
diversely by theologians, so let's leave it aside.
However, reincarnation seems more difficult to recon-
cile with Church law; it is a revival of the metempsychosis of Pythagoras.[25]

A. K.   This isn't the appropriate time to discuss a question
whose answer demands extensive development. You
will find it treated in *The Spirits' Book* and in *The*

■ ■ ■

[25] *Translator's Note: Metempsychosis: See the Glossary*

Gospel–Explained by the Spiritist Doctrine. I will touch upon it only briefly here.

The ancient theory of metempsychosis involved the transmigration of the soul of man into animal, which infers retrogradation. That theory was not widely accepted. Transmigration through the bodies of animals was not considered to be inherent in the nature of the human soul, but rather a temporary punishment for earthly sins. Souls of the lewd were thought to inhabit pigs and wild bears; souls of the inconstant and stupid, birds; and souls of the lazy and coarse, aquatic animals. After some time, determined by the soul's culpability, the soul would depart from the animal prison and return through death and rebirth to humanity. Animal incarnation was not, then, an absolute condition. As you can see, it was tied to human incarnation— so much so that it was also believed that the punishment of timid men was to inhabit the bodies of women, where they would be exposed to disdain and abuse. This notion was intended to serve as a kind of threat to the simple, rather than as an article of faith to the philosophers. Just as we tell children, "If you are bad, the big bad wolf will eat you," the ancients told criminals, "If you are bad, you will turn into a wolf," and today we say, "If you are bad, the devil will get you and drag you to hell."

The plurality of existences, according to the Spiritist Doctrine, differs fundamentally from metempsychosis in that it does not recognize incarnation of the human soul into animal bodies, even as a form of punishment. The high spirits teach that the soul does not retrogress, but always progresses. Its different bodily existences are limited to human experiences; each is a step the soul takes on the path to intellectual and ethical progress. This idea is very different from metempsychosis.

Unable to reach full development during a single existence—which, in many cases, is shortened by accidental causes—the soul is permitted by God to complete in a new incarnation those things it began in its previous one, or to correct what was done wrong the previous time. The purification in corporeal life consists of the tribulations we suffer during it.

As far as whether the plurality of existences of the soul contradicts certain Church dogmas, I will only say this: either reincarnation exists or it doesn't. If it exists, it's a law of nature. To prove that it doesn't exist, one would have to show first that it conflicts with natural law, not with religious dogma, and, second, that there exists another law that clearly and more logically explains the questions involved. Beyond that, it's easy to demonstrate that certain Church dogmas may find a rational explanation in reincarnation; the phenomenon is accepted today by those who once rejected it because they did not formerly understand it. It's not, then, a matter of denial but of reinterpretation.

Those who wish to reject our interpretation are perfectly free to do so. The idea of the plurality of existences is rapidly becoming popular, because it is extremely logical and is consistent with God's justice. Once it has been recognized as a natural truth, what will the Church do?

Briefly, reincarnation is not an imagined system to satisfy the needs of an ideal or the needs of a personal opinion. It either is or isn't a fact. If it's shown that certain human conditions are impossible without reincarnation, then it's necessary to admit that those conditions are the consequences of reincarnation. And, if it's a part of nature, it can't be annulled just by contrary opinion.

Priest   According to the spirits, is anyone who disbelieves in them or in their manifestations less fortunate in the future life?

A. K.   No. The enlightened intelligences who instruct us are not so unreasonable. They tell us that God is sovereignly just and good; God doesn't make mankind's future destiny dependent upon conditions of which it is unaware. Spirits don't teach that there is no salvation outside of Spiritist principles; rather, like Christ, they teach that outside of love (charity), there is no salvation.

Priest   Since the spirits promote only the principles of morality found in the Gospel, I don't see the usefulness of the Spiritist Doctrine; we were able to attain salvation even before this doctrine was formulated. It would be different if the spirits came to teach great new truths that might change the face of the Earth, the way Christ did. Furthermore, there are thousands of spirits who contradict each other, calling white what others say is black. As a result, their supporters have formed many sects since the beginning of time. At least Christ was alone, and his doctrine was unique. Wouldn't it be better to leave the spirits in peace and content ourselves with what we already have?

A. K.   In considering the Church as the only discerner of human knowledge, it seems to me, you show great bias. Christ spoke the truth, and the Spiritist Doctrine cannot say anything different. Rather than condemn the Spiritist Doctrine, the Church should welcome it as a powerful ally that confirms, through all the voices from beyond the grave, the fundamental truths of religion that skeptics reject. That materialism is against the Doctrine is easily explained. But that the Church aligns itself on the side of materialism and against the Spiritist Doctrine is less conceivable. The Church is equally inconsistent when it labels as diabolical a philosophy that is supported by the same authority as it is, and that proclaims the Divine mission of the founder of Christianity.

Could Christ possibly have said or revealed everything? No, since [a paraphrase of what] He himself said, *"I still have many things to tell you, but you would not understand them. This is why I speak in parables."* The Spiritist Doctrine arrives during a period when humanity is mature enough to understand it. It completes and explains what Christ intentionally left unsaid, or revealed only in allegorical form. You will say, undoubtedly, that the Church is competent to provide that explanation. Still, which one of them shall it be—Roman, Greek, or Protestant? Since they disagree with one another, each would explain it in its own way, feeling right in its explanation. Which of them would succeed in uniting all the dissidents? Foreseeing that human beings would bring their own passions and prejudices to the issue, God, in an expression of perfect wisdom, did not wish to trust them with the care of this new revelation. God gave it to the spirits, as servants of the Divine plan, to proclaim the truth throughout the world, beyond the intimate limits of any religion, so that it could be applied to all and exploited by none.

On the other hand, isn't it true that the various Christian sects have departed in some things from the path trod by Christ? Can you honestly say that His moral precepts are scrupulously observed? Haven't the various sects transformed His words so that they serve to support their own ambitions and passions? Through the voices of the spirits sent by God, the Spiritist Doctrine comes to revive the conscientious observance of Christ's precepts among those who've pushed them aside. Could this be why it's qualified by traditional Christian denominations as a satanic work?

The differing opinions among Spiritists can't be construed as "division." In the dawn of a field of study, when observations are still incomplete, it's not surprising that differing theories arise. Those differences, though, rest upon minute points rather than the fundamental principle. Certain groups may establish "schools" that explain certain facts in their own ways, but they aren't divisions any more than the different schools of thought are that divide learned women and men of sciences such as medicine and physics. Hasn't Christianity itself given birth to numerous sects since its origin? Why did the word of Christ lack sufficient power to silence all the controversies? Why is it susceptible to interpretations that still divide Christians into different churches, all claiming to possess the exclusive truth necessary for salvation, while simultaneously cordially detesting and denouncing each other in the name of their Divine master, who only preached love and charity? "Human weakness," you will answer, and you will be right. How, then, do you expect the Spiritist Doctrine to suddenly triumph over that weakness and transform human nature as if by magic?

Let's consider the question of utility. You said the Spiritist Doctrine revealed nothing new. That's a mistake. It teaches many new things to those who don't limit themselves to a superficial study. It substituted the maxim, "Outside of love (charity), there is no salvation," which unites people, for the maxim, "Outside the Church, there is no salvation," which divides them. It's the beginning of a new era for humanity.

You said that this new era could have come about without the Spiritist Doctrine. I agree. It could also have happened without many scientific discoveries. Humans certainly lived well before the discovery of new planets, before the eclipses were calculated, before the microscopic world was known, and before a hundred other things. The farmer, in order to live and grow his wheat, didn't need such knowledge;

nevertheless, no one denies that the revelation of those things broadened our knowledge and gave us a better understanding of the laws of nature. One of those laws that the Doctrine helps us understand is the world of the spirits. It teaches us about the influence of that world upon the physical realm. Even if its utility were limited to that, wouldn't such an important revelation already be great enough?

Now let's look at ethical influence. Let's assume that it teaches nothing new from this point of view. Which is the greater enemy of religion, the Spiritist Doctrine or materialism? Materialism is the greater enemy because it engenders belief in nothing. Spiritism is the negation of materialism, proving that it has no reason to exist. The Spiritist Doctrine doesn't rely on blind faith to convince the materialist that everything does not end with the body; rather, it actually shows it to him through visible, tangible facts. Isn't that at least a small service rendered to humanity and to religion? Yet that is still not everything. The certainty of the afterlife, and the vibrant picture of those who have preceded us in it, exemplify the necessity of good and the inevitable consequences of wrongdoing. This is why, without being a formal religion, the Spiritist Doctrine is related essentially to religious life. It develops religious feelings in those who lack them, and strengthens them in those who are unsure. In essence, religious people have an ally in the Spiritist Doctrine. Not the people with narrow views who only understand faith in the context of salvation and damnation, but those who view it in the context of God's unconditional love and mercy.

In brief, the Spiritist Doctrine facilitates and elevates religious ideas. It combats the abuses brought about by selfishness, greed, and ambition. After all, who would have the courage to defend such abuses when confronted with the facts presented by the Spiritist Doctrine? While the Doctrine is not indispensable to salvation, it at least facilitates it by setting us firmly on the path of good. And what sensible person would dare to assert that the Spiritist Doctrine's lack of orthodoxy is more reprehensible in the eyes of God than atheism or materialism? I pose the following questions to all those who base their arguments against the Spiritist Doctrine on its possible religious consequences:

First, *who will fare better in the afterlife, one who believes in nothing or one who believes in general truths without yielding to certain points of dogma?*

Second, *will the Protestant or anticlerical have the same fate as the atheist and the materialist?*

Third, *should a person who is not religious, yet is good and indulgent toward a neighbor and loyal in social relations, expect less salvation than a person who believes in everything, but is hard, selfish, and lacking in charity?*

Finally, which would have greater value in the eyes of God: the practice of Christian morality without the duties of religion, or the practice of religion without the duties of morality?

I have answered your questions, Reverend, and responded to the objections you presented to me, but as I told you at the outset, my purpose was to familiarize you with the Spiritist Doctrine's true aspects.

This doesn't mean we take lightly your interest. We appreciate your interest in our explanation. For us, the explanations have greater value the more freely and voluntarily they are received. We don't have the right to exercise constraint upon anyone or to infringe on the conscience of those who, having beliefs that sufficiently satisfy them, don't spontaneously seek us out. I have said that the best way to

learn about the Spiritist Doctrine is to study the theory. The facts will come afterward, naturally, and
they will be easily understood regardless of the order
in which circumstances may present them. Our publications are intended to facilitate this study. We recommend that they be read in the following order:

The first reading should be of the following summary,
which introduces the whole and outlines the most
prominent points of the Spiritist thought. With that, one
can become familiar with the Spiritist Doctrine and see
that, in essence, something serious exists there. In the
brief exposition, we try to indicate the most important
points that the observer should study. Lack of sufficient
knowledge and prejudice have been the primary reasons for erroneous opinions.

If, after this reading, one wishes to continue further,
read *The Spirits' Book,* where the principles are more
fully developed. Afterwards, read *The Mediums'
Book* for a study of the psychical phenomena, also
intended as a guide for those who wish to work by
themselves or get a better understanding of the phenomena. There are also several books that elaborate
upon the application and ethical consequences of
the doctrine, such as *The Gospel—Explained by the
Spiritist Doctrine, Heaven and Hell,* and others.

The *Revue Spirite*[26] constitutes, by the wealth of
accounts and discussions it offers, a practical course
on the Spiritist Doctrine, for it offers validation of
its theoretical and experimental precepts. It's a
pleasure for us to give any necessary explanations
to the sincere seekers, who have done some preliminary study, on any point they haven't completely
understood.

■ ■ ■

[26] *Translator's Note: See footnote 4.*

CHAPTER II

ELEMENTARY PRINCIPLES OF THE SPIRITIST DOCTRINE

1. It is wrong to believe that witnessing extraordinary phenomena is enough to convince nonbelievers. Those who don't admit to the existence of a soul or spirit within themselves, won't accept it outside of themselves either, since to deny the cause is, implicitly, to deny the effects. And those who do admit to the existence of the soul, almost always possess preconceived ideas that deter them from a serious, impartial examination of the facts. The questions and objections they raise can't be answered immediately, since each response usually requires a complete course of study. Only previous study can preclude objections that originate from ignorance of both the causes of the phenomena and the conditions in which they are produced.

2. Anyone unfamiliar with the Spiritist position supposes that the phenomena can be produced like a physics or chemistry experiment. From this misconception, they wrongly believe that spirit beings can be subjected to their will. Under these conditions, the observation method is certain to produce no valid information.[27]

    Individuals who don't accept the existence and possibility of interaction with spirits, or who don't understand either

■ ■ ■

[27] *Translator's Note: See Note 19 above (about nonexperimental methods).*

their nature or their mode of action, behave as if spirits operate on command; when such people don't receive what they request, they conclude that there are no spirits. However, if they were to adopt a different method of action, they would understand that spirits are only the souls of women and men. Since all of us will return to the spirit state after death, we should understand that, as self-conscious beings, we wouldn't want to serve as playthings to satisfy the curious.

3.   Even though certain phenomena may be induced, the fact that spirits are free individualities, masters of their wills, precludes the notion that they're at the absolute disposal of anyone who wishes. And anyone who claims he or she is able to attain them at will shows only lack of true understanding or naive belief. One must wait for the event to occur in order to systematically watch the phenomenon. Often, the most interesting and conclusive events happen when they are least expected.

Whoever seriously wants to learn, must have patience and perseverance, waiting for the right circumstances; otherwise, it's better not to bother.

4.   Meetings that have mediumistic manifestations as their sole object aren't always held under conditions conducive to obtaining satisfactory results or establishing conviction. Incredulous persons leave such meetings even more skeptical. Afterwards, they confront those who speak of the Spiritist Doctrine's serious character with the often ridiculous events they have witnessed. In this regard, they are no more logical than the person who tries to judge an artwork by the first attempts of an apprentice, or a person by his picture. Christian Spiritism, like art, also has its apprentices, and whoever wishes to be informed must learn from more than one source. Only by methodical examination and comparison can judgment be confirmed.

5.   Frivolous meetings are a serious detriment because they give a false idea of the Spiritist Doctrine's true character. Those who have attended only this kind of meeting cannot

seriously evaluate a subject treated so lightly by those who call themselves authorities. Only earnest study gives learners the ability to make informed judgments and to separate the good from the bad.

6. The same reasoning applies to those who judge the Spiritist Doctrine by reading critical books that give an incomplete and distorted idea of it. Just as poetry shouldn't be held accountable for poets who write bad verse, serious Spiritism can't be responsible for those who don't understand it or who practice it contrary to its precepts.

It's deplorable, many say, that there are so many writings that are critical of basic science; it would be preferable if all writings did justice to science. However, the worst thing is that people don't take time to read more discriminately. All the arts and sciences share that unfortunate circumstance. Aren't there error-ridden publications about even the most serious subjects?

If those who criticize the Spiritist Doctrine were to base their judgment on more than superficial impressions, they would have a more accurate understanding of what the Doctrine accepts and what it rejects, and they wouldn't associate it with ideas and practices that it firmly denies.

ABOUT THE SPIRITS

7. The spirits are not, as many people suppose, a distinct class in Creation; rather, they are the souls of those who once inhabited Earth. Whoever accepts that the soul survives after the body's death admits the existence of spirits. To deny the existence of spirits would be to deny the soul's existence.

8. There is a misconception that spirit beings are vague and indefinite, or are phosphorescent lights similar to those that hover over swampy ground at night. They are beings similar to us. Their bodies, however, are of a subtle form of energy and are invisible to us in their normal condition.

9.   When the soul is united to the body during life, it has a double covering. One is heavy, gross, and destructible— the material body. The other is ethereal, light, and inde- structible—the *perispirit*[28] (a.k.a. spiritual body).

10.   There are, then, three essential elements in humans: 1) the soul or spirit, the intelligent principle in which thought, will, and the moral sense reside; 2) the body, the material covering that establishes the spirit's relationship with the physical world; and 3) the perispirit, an energy envelope, light and imponderable which serves as a bond and a link between the spirit and the body.

11.   When the material body is worn out and can no longer function, the spirit abandons it, just as the tree sheds its bark and the snake its skin. In short, it abandons the body as one would a garment that is no longer useful. This is what we call death.

12.   Death comes only to the bodily covering abandoned by the soul. The soul retains its energy body, or perispirit.

13.   Bodily death frees the spirit from the bond that confined it to Earth and that was the source of many of its troubles. Once freed of that burden, yet still retaining the ethereal body, the spirit is able to travel through space with the speed of thought.

14.   The soul, the perispirit, and the material body together constitute a person; the soul and the perispirit, separated from the body, constitute the spirit.

Note: One may say that the spirit has a single nature, while the soul has a dual nature, and a human being has a *triple nature*.[29] It

■ ■ ■

[28] *Translator's Note: See footnote 16*

■ ■ ■

[29] *Translator's Note: It might help to think of this triad-like arrangement in terms of the structure of a peach or an apricot. At the core of these fruits, exists a nucleus, i.e., an inner germ, which we can think of as the spirit. The nucleus is surrounded by a stone or perisperm, which in us, is analogous to the perispirit. The stone, in turn, is surrounded by the edible flesh of the fruit, which is comparable to our physical body flesh.*

would be more exact to use the word spirit to designate the intelligent principle, and the term soul to designate the semimaterial being formed from the union of that principle with the energy body. Nevertheless, because the intelligent principle can hardly be conceived in isolation from some form of matter, and the spiritual body can't be conceived without the animation of the spirit, the words soul and spirit are used interchangeably.

15.   Spirits clothed in physical bodies constitute living human beings, or the visible corporeal world. Deprived of those bodies, they inhabit the spiritual or invisible world, dimensions of which exist—without our suspecting it—in the world in which we live, just as we live in the midst of infinitely small worlds, of which we were never aware before the invention of the microscope.

16.   Spirits are not, consequently, abstract entities; they are concrete and definite beings, though they need the perispirit to be perceived in the physical realm. It follows that if, at any given moment, the energy veil that apparently separates them from us were lifted, we would see that they populate the space all around us.

17.   Spirits possess all the perceptions they experienced on Earth, but on a higher level because their faculties are not weakened by matter. They have sensations unknown to us and can see and hear things that our limited senses aren't able to see or hear. For them, there is no obscurity, except among the more backward ones whose perceptions are relatively more limited.

They sense our thought stream and may be able to make out the content of our thoughts (when sufficiently advanced). Therefore, the thoughts we were able to conceal from someone during earthly life, we may no longer hide after that person's physical demise. (See also *The Spirits' Book*, question 237.)

18.   The spirits are everywhere. They are at our side, nudging us and constantly observing us. Because of their incessant presence among us, they are the agents of various phenomena. They play an important part in the mental spheres of human life, and to a certain extent, in the physical world as well. They constitute, in a manner of speaking, one of the forces of nature.

19.   Assuming that the survival of the soul or spirit is acknowledged, it is rational to believe that the feelings they have toward us persist in the afterlife; otherwise, the souls of our relatives and friends would be totally lost to us at death. Since the souls of those who loved us during earthly life continue to do so after death, and since spirit beings can go everywhere, it follows that they utilize the means available to them to come to us. Experience confirms this.

In fact, experience demonstrates that the spirits maintain the affections they established on Earth and that they take pleasure in being reunited with those they love. Likewise, they are indifferent toward those who show them indifference.

20.   The purpose of the Spiritist Doctrine is to demonstrate and study the manifestations of the spirits in order to learn about their abilities, their happy or unhappy situations, and their future. Briefly, its purpose is to provide knowledge of the spiritual world.

These verified manifestations lead to undeniable proof of the soul's existence, of its survival after bodily death, and of its individuality after death—that is, of its future life. It is the negation of materialistic theories, as much by logical reasoning as by facts.

21.   Those who are not familiar with the principles of the Spiritist Doctrine generally believe that the spirits, merely by being separated from matter, must know everything. This is a serious error. Spirits, being only the souls of men and women, don't achieve perfection immediately after leaving their bodies. Their progress is made only with time. They gradually dispose of their imperfections and acquire the knowledge they lacked on Earth.

It would be unreasonable to assume that the soul of a brute or of a criminal suddenly becomes wise and virtuous. It would also be unreasonable to suppose that, contrary to God's justice, they continue perpetually in a state of inferiority. On Earth there are people at all levels of knowledge and unawareness, of goodness and badness. The same is true in the world of the spirits. Some are merely frivolous and mischievous. Others are liars, frauds, hypocrites, wrongdoers, and full of vengeance. On the other hand, some possess the most sublime virtues and knowledge on a level unimaginable to us on Earth.

That diversity in the qualities of the spirits is one of the most important points to consider, because it explains why the nature of the communications received is sometimes good, sometimes not. It's in distinguishing the good from the bad that we must pay the closest attention. (See also *The Spirits' Book*, question 100, and *The Mediums' Book*, Chapter XXIV.)

COMMUNICATION WITH THE INVISIBLE WORLD

22.   Given the existence, survival, and individuality of the soul, we must then consider one crucial question: **Is communication possible between spirits and the living?** That possibility was proven through experience, once it was understood that there are relations between the visible and the invisible worlds, and once the cause, the nature, and the modality of these relations were known. A new field was then opened to investigation, and the key to many great problems was found. At the same time, a powerful moralizing element was established to end doubt over the afterlife.

23.   One cause of many doubts about the possibility of communications from the Beyond is a false idea many have about the soul's state after death. They imagine the soul to be a breath, a vapor, something vague and barely comprehensible, something that evaporates and departs to a distant place from which it can't return. But if we think of the soul as still united to a subtle energy body, forming with it a specific and individual being, its relations with the living are not incompatible with reason.

24. The invisible world is in perpetual interaction with the visible world. This unceasing interaction of the two suggests that there have been spirits for as long as there has been humanity. And, if these spirits have the power of manifesting themselves, then it's logical that they must have done so before, and among all peoples throughout history.

Nevertheless, in our times, the manifestations of spirits have greatly developed and acquired a more authentic character. This is because Divine Wisdom decided to end the plague of skepticism and materialism through tangible facts and evidences, permitting those who have left the Earth to return to it in order to attest to their existence, and reveal to us their happy or unhappy situations.

25. The relations between the visible and invisible worlds may be perceptible or imperceptible, spontaneous or provoked. The spirits may influence people in a hidden manner by suggesting thoughts to them and by influencing them tangibly with effects perceptible to the senses.

Spontaneous manifestations are not planned or sought by individuals. They are often produced among people unacquainted with Spiritist ideas, who, unable to explain them, attribute them to miraculous causes. On the other hand, the manifestations that are sought and planned occur through certain individuals called mediums (also known as psychics, or sensitives), who are gifted with special faculties.

26. Spirits can communicate in many different ways—by writing, drawing, making music, producing noises and movements of objects.

27. Sometimes spirits may act by moving objects or making noises. They use this means to announce their presence and call attention to themselves, just as we do when we knock to announce that somebody is at the door. Some don't limit themselves to making moderate sounds, but produce loud noises imitating dishes falling and breaking, doors that open and slam like thunder, and furniture thrown to the floor. Some cause serious disturbances and physical damage.

28. Even though it is ethereal and invisible to us in its normal state, the perispirit is made up of matter in a rarefied form. In certain cases, the spirit is able to effect a kind of molecular modification that makes it visible and even tangible. This is how apparitions are produced—a phenomenon that is no more extraordinary than when water vapor, normally invisible, becomes visible as it condenses. And when they do it, they always present themselves with the appearances they had in life, and by which they can be recognized. (See also *The Mediums' Book,* "Spontaneous Physical Manifestations," Chapter V.)

29. To see spirits regularly is very rare; however, isolated phenomena are frequent enough, particularly at the moment of death. When the spirit abandons the body, it's anxious to see its relatives and friends, and inform them that it has passed on, and also that it's still alive.

If we look back, we realize how often we have witnessed similar incidents without our perceiving them at the time. These didn't occur at midnight, in our sleep, but in daylight when we were wide awake. Such occurrences were once considered to be supernatural or miraculous and were attributed to magic or the occult. Since then, however, Spiritist knowledge has supplied the explanation for them; it is now known how such phenomena are produced and that they belong to a class of natural occurrences.

30. It was by means of the perispirit that the spirit animated its body when alive, and it's by that same means that it acts upon matter, after death, to produce sounds and to lift, drop, or transport tables and other objects. These phenomena are not so surprising, if we consider that even the most powerful motors are powered by the least dense substances, such as hydrogen, and electricity.

Also, by means of the perispirit, the spirit can direct mediums to write, speak, or draw. Lacking a physical body, the spirit operates through the medium's body to communicate. It makes the organs of expression of the medium operate by enveloping and penetrating them with a subtle energy.

31.   To produce the phenomenon of rapping tables, the spirit depends on the perispirit to move the table, either causing it to thrust or shake, or to produce intelligent raps that represent letters of the alphabet to form words and phrases. In this kind of phenomenon, the table serves only as an instrument that the spirit uses (as it does a pencil in order to write), by temporarily investing it with a spiritual kind of energy. *The spirit, however, never actually becomes a part of the objects.*

It's ridiculous for people, who are affected emotionally by the manifestation of a loved one, to embrace the table;[30] it's the same as embracing the walking stick used by someone to knock at a door. We can say the same thing about those who speak to the table as if the spirit were drawn into the wood or as if the wood had become the spirit. In communications of this type, the spirit is not within the table, but beside it, just as it would be if it were corporeal. In fact, we would see it there, if it were to become visible just then. The same is true in phenomena that involve written communications. The spirit is beside the medium, directing his or her hand or transmitting thoughts to the medium in a closed mental circuit.

When a table rises from the floor and stays in the air, it's not with muscle power that the spirit suspends it, but rather through the action of an energy field that envelopes and penetrates the table. The energy neutralizes the effects of

■ ■ ■

[30] *Translator's Note: Tables are no longer used for any kind of psychic phenomena. Other methods are considered faster and more efficient, such as automatic writing, and trance speaking.*

gravity.[31] The energy penetrating the table gives it a lower specific weight for a moment. In a way it's analogous to a vacuum chamber. Of course, these are simple comparisons, offered just to show the analogy of the effects and never the absolute similarity of the causes.

When a table moves in a certain direction, the spirit doesn't run with it, rather it remains calmly in its place and by a projection of mental force produces the necessary impulse to make the table move according to its will. Similarly, knocks heard on the table aren't made with the spirit's hand. The effect is produced by the energy activated by the spirit's will.

The phenomenon of the spirit lifting a person[32] (also known as levitation) into the air is accomplished through the same energy used to lift, transport, or throw an object. Production of these phenomena is regulated by the same law.

32. Thus, it can be seen that the Spiritist manifestations, of whatever type, are in no way miraculous or supernatural. They are phenomena produced by virtue of laws that govern the relations of the visible world with the invisible one—laws as natural as those of electricity and gravity. Spiritism is the field of knowledge that makes that law known to us, just as mechanics teaches us the laws of movement and optics those of light. Mediumistic manifestations have taken place throughout history. The law directing

■ ■ ■

[31] *Translator's Note: Daniel Dunglas Hume, a Nineteenth Century medium, became famous for the ability to produce levitation phenomena. Mr. Hume lived in England and traveled throughout Europe demonstrating his paranormal powers. Numerous incidents of levitation have been recorded in Christianity and Islam. Among the first was Simon Magus in the first century. Other incidents reported among the Roman Catholic saints include the occurrences to Joseph of Cupertino (1603–1663), and Saint Teresa of Avila (1515–1582) whom eyewitness confirmed levitated a foot and a half off the ground for about a half hour (Underhill, Evelyn "Mysticism," 1955).*

■ ■ ■

[32] *For a more detailed explanation see The Mediums' Book, "Theory of Physical Manifestations," Chapter IV.*

them, once known, explains many problems once considered unsolvable; it's the key to a multitude of phenomena
that have been exploited and exaggerated by superstition.

33.　Once the aura of miracle working is completely removed,
Spiritist phenomena aren't difficult to understand,
because they take place among other natural phenomena.
In the past, all phenomena stemming from unidentified
causes were considered supernatural. However, scientific
discoveries have gradually reduced the circle of the
miraculous, which has been further shrunk by the discovery of the new principles revealed by the Spiritist
Doctrine. Therefore, those who accuse Spiritism of reviving interest in miracles only prove they speak about matters they don't understand.

34.　Spirit manifestations are of two kinds: those of *physical
effects* and those of *intelligent communications*. Physical
effects are material phenomena, such as movements,
sounds, transportation of objects, and so forth. Intelligent
communications consist of the regular exchange of
thoughts by means of signs or words, and, frequently, this
exchange is carried out in writing.

35.　The communications we receive from the spirits may be
good or bad, accurate or false, profound or frivolous,
depending upon the nature of those who are manifesting.
Those who give proof of wisdom and scholarship are spirits advanced along the path of progress. Those who show
themselves to be rude and ill-natured are those who are
still backward, but who will develop with time.

Spirits can only reliably address questions regarding issues
with which they are already acquainted and that are within
their level of advancement. They are also restricted by the
limited scope of things they are permitted to tell us; there
are things they may not reveal because it's not the appropriate time for humanity to know.

36.　From the diversity of qualities and aptitudes among spirit
beings, it follows that it's not sufficient to address our-

selves to any one individuality to obtain a reliable answer to a particular question. A spirit being may give us its personal opinion only, which may not be worth much. If the spirit is prudent, it'll acknowledge its limited knowledge about things with which it's not familiar. If it's a frivolous or deceiving spirit, it'll answer in any manner it chooses, with no regard for truth. If it's conceited, it'll present its opinions as absolute truth. It's because of this that St. John the Evangelist said, "Dear friends, do not believe every spirit, but test the spirits to see whether they are from God, because many false prophets have gone out into the world."[33]

Experience reveals the wisdom of John's advice. It's imprudent and frivolous to accept, without examination, everything that the spirits reveal. It's necessary to be thoroughly familiar with the character and experience of those with whom we are in contact. (See also *The Mediums' Book*, Chapter XXIV, item 267.)

37. Spirits are often recognized by the quality of their language. The language of truly good and more advanced spirits is always dignified, noble, logical, and without contradiction. In it, one senses wisdom, benevolence, modesty, and virtue. Their language is concise and stripped of redundancies. On the other hand, the language of inferior, coarse, or proud spirits is a vacuum of ideas filled with an abundance of words. Every false thought, every statement contrary to a pure morality, any and all ridiculous advice, all gross, trivial, or frivolous expressions—in short, all manifestations of malevolence, presumption, or ignorance—are undeniable signs of inferior spirits.

38. Inferior, or unevolved, spirits have little knowledge. Their horizon is limited and their insight restricted. They often have false or incomplete ideas about things, and furthermore, they are still dominated by their earthly prejudices,

■ ■ ■

[33] *Translator's Note: 1 John 4:1.*

which renders them incapable of addressing certain questions thoughtfully. As a result, they can lead us into error, intentional or not, about matters even they don't fully understand.

39.   Not all unevolved spirits are essentially ill-meaning. Some are merely unaware and shallow. Others are witty and entertaining, and are sophisticated in sarcastic satire. In the spiritual world, as on Earth, we encounter every kind of character flaw and all levels of intellectual and moral superiority.

40.   Superior spirits concern themselves only with intelligent communications that enlighten us. Physical or purely material phenomena are more often the work of lower-level spirits. In the spirit world, the strenuous tasks are performed by the less skilled, not by the learned, so to speak.

41.   We must always be calm and collected when communicating with the spirits. We should never forget that they are the souls of women and men and it's wrong to treat their efforts as a pastime or entertainment. If we show respect for one's mortal remains, we should show even greater respect for the spirit. Frivolous meetings lacking in serious objectives fall short of that obligation. People who hold such meetings forget that one day they'll be in the spirit realm themselves and won't appreciate being treated with so little regard.[34]

42.   Another equally essential point to consider is that the spirits are free and communicate only with those they wish, and when their activities and desires permit it; they aren't subject to our whims. No one can force them to

■ ■ ■

[34] *Translator's Note: Meetings conducted with futile intent are indeed damaging to the image and credibility of the Doctrine, and detrimental to their participants. With rare exceptions, the readings provided add nothing to the person's growth. Queries on wedding prospects, real estate transactions, travel opportunities, and other akin themes are never answered by the more experienced and morally superior spirits. Respect, faith, introspection, and prayer are conditions* sine qua non *for effective interaction with the spirit world.*

manifest themselves when they don't want to, or force them to tell anything they find inappropriate. Therefore, no one can boast that a certain spirit will answer him or her at any given moment or will reply to any given question. Making such an assertion shows an ignorance of the principles that govern the relationship with the spirit-world; only charlatans assume results 100% of the time.

43. Spirits are attracted to those who want their presence because of a similarity in values, character, and intentions. Just as a wise man doesn't frequent gatherings of playful youth, high-minded spirits don't usually assist at trivial meetings. Common sense tells us this. If they do attend those meetings, their only purpose is to give beneficial advice, correct faults, and redirect the wayward onto the right path. If they are unheeded, they leave.

It's erroneous to think that serious spirits will reply to the useless and idle questions of those who show little respect or affection toward them, demonstrating no desire for instruction. Enlightened spirits don't meddle in the ordinary events of our lives, nor occupy themselves with curiosity seekers. They wouldn't have done so when they were incarnate and won't do so now.

44. The result of frivolous meetings is the attraction of frivolous spirits who only look for opportunities to show off and deceive. Sensible women and men prefer gatherings that offer opportunities for self-improvement for the same reason that learned spirits attend only serious meetings. Elevated spirits give instructions only in meetings where the objective is learning, rather than satisfying mere curiosity.

45. From the preceding point, it is evident that to be successful, every Spiritist meeting must be primarily serious in character, and proceed with respect, religiosity, and dignity, if its goal is to obtain the habitual cooperation of good spirits. It shouldn't be forgotten that had those same spirits introduced themselves when they were incarnate, they would've been treated with proper courtesy, and they have an even greater right to that courtesy after leaving their physical bodies.

46. It is wrongfully claimed that certain curious, frivolous, and entertaining experiments are useful in convincing disbelievers. The results suggest otherwise. The unbeliever, already disposed toward showing little regard for the most sacred beliefs, is unable to see anything meaningful in what others ridiculed, nor can he respect what is presented to him without the proper regard. Therefore, he leaves with a negative impression from meetings where order, discipline, and high purposes are lacking.

Above all, what convinces a unbeliever is proof of the presence of those whose memories are dear to him. It is his loved one's serious, solemn comments and intimate revelations that move him. Because he has respect, veneration, and love for the person whose soul comes to communicate, the unbeliever is shocked and feels scandalized if his loved one is called into an irreverent gathering, characterized by dancing tables and the scribbling of playful spirits. Unbelieving as he is, his conscience repels the alliance of the serious with the profane. Therefore, he calls all that a sham and often leaves less convinced than when he arrived.

Meetings of that kind always do more harm than good, because they cause more people to reject the phenomenon than to accept it. In addition, such meetings establish motives and opportunities for ridicule, making the Spiritist Doctrine vulnerable to the criticism of detractors.

47. Anyone who considers the phenomena of physical manifestations a plaything is in error. Physical manifestations may not be as important as instructions on ethical behavior and spiritual matters, but they are useful because they offer the tangible material preferred by physical science. And, although they are less necessary today, they still help some people towards conviction. Therefore, order and respect are required at experimental meetings. Meetings so conducted produce phenomena more reliably and convince non believers more effectively.

48. Some people have a very mistaken idea about spirit communication. They think calling upon the spirits consists of summoning up the dead from the tomb with doleful pageantry. The little we have said on this subject should have corrected any such error. Only in novels, on the stage, and in fantastic stories do the dead come forth from sepulchers wrapped in shrouds and rattling bones. The Spiritist Doctrine, which has never performed miracles, isn't involved in such nonsense and has never claimed to revive a dead body. Once a body is in the tomb, it will never come out of it again. The soul is not encumbered with the material covering of the body from which it separated at the moment of death. Once that separation is effected, there is no longer any common bond between the spirit and the body.

49. Malicious criticism has represented Spiritist communications as a ridiculous mixture of superstition, magical practices, and necromancy. If those who speak so naively of the Spiritist Doctrine had studied it, they would have spared themselves from such wild imagination, which only serves to prove their ignorance and ill will.

To people who are strangers to the field, it's our duty to say that in order to communicate with the spirits, there's no day, hour, or place that is more opportune than any other. No formulas, or sacramental or cabalistic words exist, no preparation or initiation is needed to make contact with the spirit realm. The use of any sign or material object to attract or repel them has no effect whatsoever; thought alone is sufficient.

Mediums receive communications from the spirits in a normal state of consciousness, as simply and naturally as if they were uttered by living persons. The interaction with the spirits must be conducted with respect and in the name of God. Respect is a prerequisite for serious people who wish to contact enlightened spirits. Only the phony employ flashy routines and accessories.

THE PURPOSE OF COMMUNICATION

50.   The providential purpose of spirit communication is to give believers a more exact idea of the future and to convince the incredulous that everything does not end for humanity at the end of earthly life. The good spirits come to instruct us for our betterment and advancement, and not to reveal to us what we shouldn't yet know or what must be attained through our own efforts.

If it were possible to interrogate the spirits to obtain solutions to all scientific questions or to make discoveries and lucrative inventions, every uneducated person could become smart without studying and every lazy person rich without working. This is not what Providence intends. Through subtle inspiration, knowledgeable spirits may help the person of character but don't exempt that person from work or study. Their rewards are the fruits of their efforts.

51.   Whoever sees spirits as lackeys of psychic readers and fortune-tellers has a very incorrect idea about them. The wise ones refuse to be bothered with useless things. Frivolous and foolish spirits, on the other hand, will deal with everything, reply to everything, and predict everything, totally disregarding the truth. They take pleasure in sowing confusion among gullible people. Therefore, it is essential to understand perfectly the kinds of questions that should be directed to the spirits. (See also *The Mediums' Book*, Chapter XXVI, item 286.)

52.   Instructions from spirits should always be treated with reserve and discernment, especially when they are presented as revelation. There is never final truth in spirit instructions. Mediums who are fascinated with themselves and value too much the attention of pseudo-intellectual spirits create troublesome situations. What's more, they waste the time and opportunity to enjoy the fruits of richer spiritual knowledge offered by good spirits.

53. Interactions with the spirit realm are not meant to serve material interests, but rather to serve our personal and moral development. If they have no other result than to reveal a new law of nature—to demonstrate the existence of the soul and its immortality—that's quite a lot, since that alone has opened a new path of human knowledge.

ABOUT MEDIUMS

54. There is a wide variety in the individual aptitudes of mediums, making them more or less suited for producing certain kinds of phenomena or receiving certain kinds of communication. According to these aptitudes, we categorize them as mediums of physical effects or of intelligent communications, such as seeing, hearing, or speaking, painting, speaking languages, writing poetry or music, etc. We must not expect more from mediums than the limits of their abilities allow. Without prior knowledge of the categories of mediumistic aptitudes, the sincere student is unable to understand certain difficulties or impossibilities encountered in practice. (See also *The Mediums' Book,* Chapter XVI, item 185.)

55. Physical effect mediums are particularly adept at producing material phenomena, such as movements or raps, using tables and other objects. When these phenomena reveal a thought or obey a will, they are intelligent effects that denote an intelligent cause.

Answers of "yes" or "no," or the indication of letters to form words and phrases, are obtained by means of a previously conventionalized number of raps. However, this primitive method is very slow and doesn't facilitate more meaningful communications. Rapping tables merely marked the beginnings of the field. Today there are means of communication available as rapid and complete as those among incarnate beings, so that nobody bothers now with those early methods.

56. Of all the methods of communicating, writing is the simplest, most rapid, and convenient. It allows the greatest flexibility and is the most commonly used.

57. In the beginning, mediums used material objects provided with a pencil (such as planchettes and similar devices). (See also *The Mediums' Book,* Chapter XIII, starting at item 152.) Much later, it was recognized that these accessories weren't needed because mediums could write directly with their hand, as in normal circumstances.

58. The medium writes under the influence of a spirit being; the medium functions as an instrument. Her hand is driven by an involuntary movement, which she can't control. Certain mediums are not aware of what they write; others are more or less vaguely aware, even if the thought is unfamiliar to them. This is what distinguishes automatic from intuitive mediums. The Spiritist Doctrine explains the process by which the spirit transmits thought to the medium and the part played by the medium in the communication. (See also *The Mediums' Book,* Chapter XIX, starting at item 223.)

59. Mediums are only accessories in communications with the spirits; effective communication depends upon the will of the spirits. If they don't wish to communicate, the medium will receive nothing—becoming like a musical instrument without a musician. Spirits communicate when they want to, or are able to. *No medium has the power to force spirits to present themselves.* This explains the unsteadiness of results, and the lapses mediums suffer. It would be wrong, then, to consider mediumship a skill. Skill is acquired by effort; whoever develops a skill is always its master. The medium is never a master of his or her faculty because their success depends upon the will of another.

60. Mediums of physical effects, e.g., movement of objects, who produce certain phenomena regularly and at will, are associated with spirits of lower development that take pleasure in exhibitions of this kind.[35] However, it is flawed to assume that these spirits, undeveloped as they may be, would simply stage farces.

61. We know that some chemicals can't be combined in the presence of light, and that light affects the reactions of other chemicals. Likewise, all Spiritist phenomena are the result of combining the energies of the spirit and the medium. It's not surprising that, in certain circumstances, that combination is hampered by the presence of light.

62. Intelligent communications take place as a result of the spirit exerting influence upon the medium, which requires a rapport between their energies. Thus, the ease of the manifestations depends upon the affinity of the two kinds of energy. Therefore, each medium is apt to receive thoughts from certain spirits. And just as a medium may be a good instrument for one spirit, they may be a very poor one for another. Because of this, a spirit, encountering two equally gifted mediums, might communicate well through one and not the other.

63. It's incorrect to think that every medium can receive, with equal facility, communications from any spirit. No medium can obtain communications at will, nor can they produce all the phenomena.

The spirits prefer to seek out and use as instruments those mediums who are the most compatible with them. To impose upon the spirits the first medium at hand would be the same as requiring a pianist to play violin under the assumption that, because he knows music, he can play any instrument.

■ ■ ■

[35] *Translator's Note: Experience accumulated in the last thirty years suggest that some of the phenomena that early on were characterized as mediumistic, i.e., depending on the assistance of spirits, are effectively the result of human mental powers, e.g., clairvoyance, remote viewing, metal bending, movement of physical objects.*

64. Affinity makes the harmonization of energies possible—communication is impossible without it. Without affinity, i.e., medium and spirit in the same mental frequency, there is no reliable communication. In the event that the expected spirit is not able to communicate, it may happen that a spirit of lower degree, often of a mischievous nature, takes its place, if the medium is not well centered. The message will tend, then, to be of little value, and often devoid of truth.

65. Affinity is sometimes impossible between certain spirits and certain mediums. At other times—and this is more commonly the case—affinity building is a very gradual process. Spirits often communicate most easily through the medium with whom they are most accustomed. This is demonstrated by the fact that the first communications with a particular spirit are usually more restrained and less explicit than later ones.

66. Energy affinity is necessary in all interactions—from table-tilting to writing—since, whatever the means of communication, the basic element is always thought.

67. In trying to make contact with a spirit being, the medium can't be assigned beforehand; the spirit makes the choice. In all cases, the medium must create a good rapport with the spirit, through meditation and prayer, either a few minutes or several days prior to the communication. This preparation helps to lessen the difficulty in initiating communications.

68. When the level of affinity is not sufficient for the spirit to communicate directly, it may do so through the medium's spiritual guide. In that case, the thought arrives second-hand—that is, it passes through two transmitters. It is clear, then, how important it is for the medium to be well assisted.

Here, the personal qualities, i.e., values, attitudes, behavior, of the medium play a very important part, because they determine the kinds of spirits he attracts to himself on a regular basis. Even the most unworthy mediums may possess powerful abilities; however, the most reliable mediums are those who combine that power with the best allies in the spiritual world. It's not the impressive names used by the spirits who sign the communication that show that kind of affinity, but rather the consistently good content of the communication itself.

69. Whether one participates or is merely an observer of another's experiments, it's essential to know how to distinguish between the different kinds of spirits that may intervene. It's also important to understand the mechanisms of all the phenomena, the conditions in which they can be produced, and the obstacles that may hinder them, in order not to waste time by asking the impossible. It's equally necessary to understand the requirements and risks of mediumship, the influence of the environment, the influence of one's moral dispositions, and so forth. (See also *The Mediums' Book*, Part II.)

THE RISKS OF MEDIUMSHIP

70. One of the greatest dangers of mediumship is spiritual obsession[36] —the fascination that some spirits exert over mediums—wherein a spirit, perhaps under a fictitious name, heavily influences the medium's will and insulates the medium from freely interacting with other sources. This danger also threatens every inexperienced student who, unaware of such a possibility, may be misled by appearances in the same way that someone unfamiliar with medicine might be deceived about the cause and nature of a disease.

Careful and constant study is indispensable to both participants and mediums, as it helps prevent many disagreeable consequences. Once again, it is necessary to recommend that study and preparation precede practice. (See also *The Mediums' Book*, Chapter XXIII.)

■ ■ ■

[36] *Translator's Note: Spiritual Obsession: See glossary*

71.   Obsessions occur in three very characteristic degrees: *simple spiritual obsession, obsessional fascination, and subjugation.*

In *simple obsession,* the medium is perfectly aware that he or she is receiving nothing good. They're not deluded about the nature of the spirits who insist on communicating and wish that they would go away. This situation isn't serious; it's simply an inconvenience that the medium can stop by breaking the mental reception or quitting writing. The spirit will tire of being ignored and leave.

Obsessional fascination is more serious because the medium is deluded. The spirit influencing the medium telepathically takes advantage of that person's trust to the point of altering a judgment about the communications received, thus leading the medium to accept great absurdities as truth. The distinctive characteristic of this type of obsession is the medium's inability or unwillingness to critically evaluate the information received. The medium genuinely believes that what he or she writes or says is just and true. The medium rejects and considers as spiteful any critical observation, and eventually breaks with friends who try to bring awareness to the problem. The medium becomes jealous of other mediums whose communications are more highly esteemed. He or she tries to assume a prominent role in meetings, but leaves if sufficient recognition is not given. Such an influence by the spirit may ultimately lead the hapless medium into the most ridiculous and compromising situations.

72.   Imposition is a distinctive characteristic of ill-minded spirits. They command and want to be obeyed. Good spirits never impose themselves; they give advice and if it's not heeded, they leave. The effects produced on us by mean entities are always upsetting, fatiguing, and generally disagreeable, causing agitation and brusque, disordered actions. Good spirits, on the other hand, leave us feeling calm, centered, and pleasant.

73. *Obsessional subjugation,* also referred to as possession, is exercised by spirits of the lowest order. Such domination can go so far as to neutralize the free will of the subject. Sometimes it is limited simply to very depressing feelings; however, it often induces awkward actions, foolish acts, shouts, and offensive or incoherent words. The afflicted individual may understand that these acts are ridiculous, but is unable to control them. This state differs drastically from mental illness, with which it is often confused. Unlike mental illness, obsessional subjugation has no organic cause. Since the causes are different, so are the forms of treatment. Aggressive medical procedures, may produce actual mental illness, where before only a psychological problem existed.

74. With mental illness, the cause of the problem is internal, so it is important to restore the individual to a healthy physical condition. With subjugation, however, the cause is external. The sick person's mind is beset by an external agent. The cure requires opposing its energy, not with material remedies, but with a superior mental force. This is very different from exorcism. So-called exorcism never produces satisfactory results; it is more likely to aggravate, rather than alleviate, the situation.

By identifying the true cause of the symptoms, the Spiritist Doctrine is able to provide the means of combating the problem. The therapy involves counseling the spirit being to reform its views and soften its feelings. Accomplishing this, the spirit voluntarily ceases the attacks and the person then becomes free and cured. (See also *The Mediums' Book,* Chapter XXV, item 279.)

75. Obsessional subjugation ordinarily affects one individual; however, a multitude of malevolent spirits imposing themselves upon a group of people can resemble a mass illness. Such a phenomenon was witnessed during Christ's life[37]—

only a superior moral power was able to subdue those malevolent beings, then called demons, and restore calm to their victim.

76. An important fact to be considered is that obsession, whatever its nature, is independent from mediumship and is encountered in all forms in a large number of people who never even heard of the Spiritist Doctrine.[38] Spirits have always existed and have always exercised their influence. Mediumship is not a cause of that influence, but simply a means of channeling it.

One can affirm, thus, that two possible outcomes are associated with the presence of a besetting entity. If the person doesn't have psychic sensitivity, the malevolent influence may turn out in some form of an unexplained illness (mental, but occasionally with physical repercussion) in the body, that escapes the limits of medicine. However, if the person has sensitivity, he or she will suffer the disturbing influence in a direct manner. The influence will be felt in the most common acts of her/his life. Mediumship only reveals the enemy's presence.

77. Those who reject everything that doesn't affect the five senses, don't admit that the spirit realm exists. However, when science becomes less centered on matter, it, too, will recognize in the invisible world surrounding us, forces

■ ■ ■

[37] *Translator's Note: Mark 1:25 ("'Be quiet!' said Jesus sternly, 'Come out of him!' The evil spirit shook the man violently and came out of him with a shriek."); Mark 5:8–10 ("For Jesus had said to him, 'Come out of this man, you evil spirit!' Then Jesus asked him, 'What is your name?' 'My name is Legion,' he replied, 'for we are many.' And he begged Jesus again and again not to send them out of the area.")*

■ ■ ■

[38] *Translator's Note: Spiritual obsession is a phenomenon that occurs independent of one's religious orientation and context. The Bible is a rich depository of cases. Examples are also documented throughout the history of the churches, and in annals of medical science. Such conditions have happened before the appearance of the Spiritist Doctrine, and will continue to happen until human kind has attained a much higher stage of spiritual and moral development.*

that exert influence upon the physical, as well as the mental, dimensions of our lives. A new road to progress will open up, and natural science will have a key for explaining many phenomena that are now little understood.

78. Since a spiritual obsession is never the doing of a good spirit, it is essential to know how to recognize the nature of the spirit being involved. A poorly prepared medium can be fooled by appearances, but one who is well prepared can recognize even the slightest suspicious sign, and the spirit, seeing that it can do nothing, leaves. Knowing beforehand how to distinguish good spirits from bad ones is indispensable to the medium who doesn't want to be deceived. It is also necessary for the simple observer, who can, with that knowledge, appreciate the value of what he or she sees and hears. (See also *The Mediums' Book,* Chapter XXIV.)

PERSONAL QUALITIES OF MEDIUMS

79. The psychic faculty is a property of the human organism and its presence doesn't depend on the moral qualities of the medium. We see the faculty in both the worthy and the unworthy. The same is not true, however, of the preference that good spirits show toward the medium.

80. Good spirits communicate when there is affinity between their energy and that of the medium and when the medium is receptive. *It must be noticed, however, that the quality of a medium is not determined by the ease with which he receives a communication. Instead, it is defined by his aptitude to cooperate with noble spirits and insulate himself from the frivolous and deceiving ones.*

81. Mediums who are less principled sometimes receive excellent communications from what can only be good spirits, but this fact shouldn't be surprising. Good spirits often communicate through such mediums for the purpose of imparting wise advice to them. If the mediums disregard the advice, they add to their own problems. God, whose goodness is infinite, can't refuse assistance to those who are most in need of it. Good spirits who try to help misguided mediums, do what missionaries do in trying to change the dispositions of spoiled people.

Good spirits, wishing to offer positive encouragement to people, sometimes avail themselves of whatever instrument is at hand; however, when they find affinity with a medium who welcomes their advice, they put the first medium aside. When the good spirits quit coming, the door is left open to those who care little about the principles of the medium. The result is that morally flawed mediums—those unconcerned with their spiritual reform—sooner or later become the prey of unprincipled spirits who lead them to bad decisions and much suffering, even in earthly life. Their faculty, which was so beautiful at the beginning and should have remained so, becomes perverted by the abandonment of the righteous company, and it gradually withers.

82. Even mediums of greater merit are not entirely protected from ill-minded spirits. There are two reasons for this. First, there isn't a person among us who is so perfect as to possess no weaknesses by which ill-meaning spirits might gain access. Second, our guides sometimes actually permit the approach of wrongdoing entities for the purpose of helping us learn discernment, i.e., to distinguish truth from error and to be on guard against accepting, at face value, everything that comes from the spirit realm. Enlightened beings never deceive us; deception, however it is received, always comes from a lower source. These deceptions may be a test of strength and preparedness for the medium; those who become discouraged reveal that they may not be instruments upon which the good spirits can depend.

83. It shouldn't be surprising to see persons of merit targeted by mean spirits, when on Earth, we also see good women and men stalked by those who aren't good. It is noteworthy that, after the publication of *The Mediums' Book*, the number of disturbed mediums greatly declined. The mediums, forewarned, became vigilant and scrutinized the slightest indications of the presence of deceiving spirits. Most of those who were victims of an obsession either did not invest in the study of the subject, as recommended, or disregarded the advice they received.

84.   Mediums are distinguished by the excellence of their extrasensory talent. In this regard, they may be more or less gifted, or more or less developed. The secure medium, the one who really qualifies as a good medium, is the one who uses his or her faculty to serve as an appropriate interpreter for the good spirits. A medium's aptitude to attract good spirits and repel bad ones results from moral superiority—the same quality that defines a good person. It is through that trait that he or she wins the friendship of good spirits and exercises ascendance over bad ones.

85.   By a similar process, the character flaws of a medium bring him/her closer to the nature of bad spirits; their imperfections deprive them of sufficient moral strength to keep the bad spirits away. *Instead of making their strength felt by these spirits, they suffer the spirits' imposition.* This applies not only to mediums, but to everyone else as well, since we are all subject to the influence of the spirits (see items 74 and 75 above).

86.   In order to impose themselves upon mediums, bad spirits skillfully exploit all of their weaknesses. Among all of mankind's flaws, pride usually presents the greatest opportunity. It's the dominant trait found in most mediums in the trough of a spiritual obsession. Conceit causes mediums to think of themselves as infallible, and therefore, to refuse all advice. A medium only needs to show unusual ability to become sought after and flattered. Unfortunately, pride is stimulated by praise, and an exaggerated sense of self-importance may lead mediums to believe that they are indispensable. The result is that such vanity jeopardizes the medium's talent.

87.   Unprepared mediums are proud of the illustrious names
(often of doubtful authenticity) signed to communications
they receive, and consider themselves the privileged interpreters of celestial powers. Good mediums, on the other
hand, think of themselves as unworthy of such favor. They
always have a healthy mistrust of the merit they receive
and critically examine everything they produce. They
know that it would be ridiculous to believe absolutely in
the names assumed by the spirits. In addition, good mediums realize they are only passive instruments and understand that good results do not confer personal merit upon
them any more than bad results are directly their responsibility. They let other unbiased persons judge their work
and are not offended by any criticism, just as actors are not
offended by criticism of the play they interpret. Simplicity
and modesty are distinctive characteristics of good mediums They are happy with the faculties they possess, not
because it elevates their importance, but because it allows
them to be useful. They are glad to be useful when the
occasion permits, but don't become annoyed when others
are preferred over them.

Mediums are the intermediaries and transmitters for the
spirits (similar to a smart telephone). It's the duty of both
the one who calls upon the spirits, and of the simple
observer, to evaluate the medium's merit as an instrument on the basis of the quality of the communications
they receive.

88.   Like all other faculties, mediumship is a gift that can be
employed for good or for hurtful ends. Its purpose is to
put us in direct contact with the souls of those who have
lived before, so that we may be able to receive teachings
and instructions about the afterlife. Just as sight enables
us to interpret the physical world, mediumship enables
us to interpret the invisible world. Those who make use of
it for their own spiritual advancement, and that of their
brothers and sisters, carry out a true mission and will be
rewarded. Those who misuse it, and employ it to satisfy

material interests by diverting it from its providential end, will sooner or later suffer the consequences, as with any person who abuses any power.

CHARLATANISM

89. Certain spirit manifestations can be faked; however, in spite of such exploitation by fake mediums, it's absurd to believe that authentic phenomena don't exist, that all spirit phenomena are the product of trickery. Anyone who has studied them, and understands the conditions for dependable communications, can easily distinguish imitation from reality. Imitations are never satisfying and deceive only the unaware, who aren't capable of recognizing the nuances that characterize the true phenomena.

90. The manifestations most easily imitated are physical effects—movements, raps, transports, direct writing—and banal answers, for which only skill and creativity are required. However, to fake communications of sublime consequence, an in-depth education, exceptional intellectual capacity, and an extraordinary ability to improvise are necessary—a combination that hardly goes with fakery.

91. Those who are unfamiliar with Christian Spiritism are generally suspicious of the good faith of mediums. Only study and experience can furnish the means for certifying the authenticity of the facts presented by mediums; lacking such knowledge, the best guarantee one can get is the medium's integrity and his or her lack of ulterior motives for personal gain. There are persons who, due to their positions and personal character, are above any suspicion. On the other hand, given that profit is a motive for fraud, good sense dictates that charlatans won't be found where they have nothing to gain. (See also *The Mediums' Book,* Chapter XXVIII.)

92. Among the Spiritist Doctrine's followers there are unreasoning enthusiasts and fanatics, just as there are everywhere else. Generally, they are its worst promoters because their eagerness to accept any paranormal phenomena at face value arouses mistrust. Trustworthy Spiritists resist the enthusiasm that blinds reason. They observe with cool calmness, avoiding the trap of illusions. Good faith aside, the novice must, before everything else, evaluate the character of those with whom he or she is in contact.

IDENTITY OF SPIRITS

93.   Since the spirits exhibit all the same traits as humanity, there must be tricksters and liars among them. Some are not in the least hesitant to present themselves under the most respectable names for the purpose of inspiring greater confidence. We shouldn't blindly accept the authenticity of their signatures.

94.   Confirming a spirit's identity is one of the greatest difficulties of experimental meetings. Often it's impossible to verify identification information, especially of more evolved spirits who lived in remote eras. Among those who communicate, many don't have names recognizable to us; to give us a point of reference, they may assume the name of an individuality with similar characteristics who is better known. For example, if a spirit uses the name of Peter, the Apostle, this is not proof of the communicant actually being that apostle—it may be him or another spirit of the same order, or perhaps one serving as his messenger. Identity confirmation is impossible and the matter becomes entirely secondary. It would be childish to attribute importance to it, since the nature, and only the nature, of the teaching is what matters—is it good or bad, worthy or unworthy of the personage whose name is assigned to it?

95.   It is easier to verify identity when dealing with contemporary individuals—those with known traits and habits—because those qualities reveal often incontestable identity. When we call upon a relative or friend, it is very natural to try to verify the identity. The means employed by those unacquainted with the Spiritist Doctrine, however, are seldom sufficient and can lead to error.

96. The spirit being reveals its identity in the communications, through its habits, character, language, and even familiar phrases. The spirit's loved ones, who share intimate details with it, provide the best confirmation. It is rare, however, that direct questions are answered, especially if they are asked by indifferent or curious people whose only purpose is to test the communicant. The spirit proves its identity—if it so desires and is able to—according to the faculty of its interpreter. When the conditions are correct and the medium is qualified, the confirmatory evidence is usually ample and satisfying. The error is in expecting the spirit to provide proof in a particular manner. (See also *The Mediums' Book,* Chapter XXIV.)

CONTRADICTIONS

97. The contradictions frequently noted in the spirits' language surprise only those with an incomplete knowledge of the Spiritist literature. Such contradictions are a result of the very nature of the spirits, whose knowledge, as we have said, depends on their level of advancement. In fact, many of them know even less than some incarnate people. On many matters, they only express their personal opinions, which may be more or less correct. Some reflect earthly prejudices they still retain. Others create their own hypotheses about still unknown facts, particularly regarding scientific questions and the origins of things. It shouldn't be surprising that they aren't always in agreement.

98. Some people are astonished to find contradictory communications signed with the same name. Only inferior spirits change their opinions according to the circumstances of their communications; superior spirits never contradict themselves. However uninitiated someone may be into the mysteries of the spiritual world, they learn how easily cer-

tain spirits adopt different names to give greater weight to
their words. Thus, it should be obvious that of two radically different communications claiming the same author-
ship, at least one must be a fraud.

99.   There are two ways to settle conflicting statements. The
first is to submit all communications to the critical examination of reason, good sense, and logic. All good spirits
recommend this. The unenlightened, however, don't—
they stand to lose credibility from such examination,
therefore, they avoid discussion and want to be believed
on their word. The second method is by corroboration
with other communications. When the same principle is
taught in many places by different spirits, through mediums unknown to each other and under diverse influences, it may be concluded that such a principle is closer
to the truth than one that originates from only one source
and is contradicted by most others. (See also *The Mediums'
Book*, Chapter XXVII, and *The Gospel-Explained by the
Spiritist Doctrine*, Introduction.)

WORTH OF THE SPIRITIST DOCTRINE

100.   Confronted by differences in the assertions made by spirits, the skeptic person may ask, "What is the purpose,
then, of studying the Spiritist Doctrine?"

The purpose is to prove, objectively, the existence of the
spirit world. The spiritual world is comprised of the souls
of humans who have lived. Recognition of that fact
results in proof of the soul's existence and its ability to
survive the body.

Souls manifesting themselves reveal the joys and sufferings they undergo in the invisible world, which are determined by the way they spent their earthly lives. In this,
we have evidence of future punishments and rewards. By
describing their state and situation to us, the spirits rectify
false ideas about the afterlife and the nature and duration
of punishments. The afterlife thus passes from a vague

and uncertain theory to a known and positive fact. Consequently, it becomes clear that we need to work the hardest during the present life, which is of short duration, toward the benefits of the future life, which is everlasting.

Let's suppose that a twenty-year-old man is certain he will die at twenty-five. What will he do during those last five years? Will he work toward the future? Certainly not. He'll try to enjoy everything in life, believing there is no advantage to working hard and denying himself anything. On other hand, if he had the certainty he'd live to the age of eighty, he'd understand the necessity of working hard and sacrificing some rest now to secure his retirement years later. The same is true of the person who is certain about the afterlife.

People who doubt the afterlife tend to devote themselves to pleasures of the moment. Worldly possessions gain undue importance, and in their wake come envy and greed. From greed, it is a short step to coveting, at any price, a neighbor's possessions; and from there come hatreds, quarrels, court claims, wars, and all the other troubles brought about by unrestrained self-interest.

Possessed by doubt about the afterlife and depressed by hopelessness and misfortune, a person sees death as the end of their sufferings. Expecting nothing after death, they may hasten the approach of that end by committing suicide. It is natural for a person without hope for the future to become desperate about the circumstances of earthly life, even to the point of mental disease in some extreme cases.

Without a belief in the future life, the present becomes humanity's primary concern, subordinating everything else. People struggle to enjoy material possessions and human honors at all costs, aspiring to elevate themselves above others and to eclipse their neighbors with their pomp and position. They attach great importance to personal image, status, and all the effects of vanity, because they can see nothing beyond those earthly concerns.

The certainty of the afterlife and its consequences changes humanity's priorities and sheds a new light on things, revealing an immense, splendid horizon. Compared to the infinity and grandeur of life beyond the grave, earthly life is a mere second in the calculation of the centuries, a grain of sand next to a mountain. Once we realize that fact, earthly goals become less significant, and we are astonished at having given importance to so many short-lived and childish things. In the middle of life's tribulations, a peace comes over us that already constitutes a level of happiness compared to the turmoil we experience when our goal is solely to elevate ourselves above others. At the same time, we are suddenly able to adopt a healthy indifference toward the situations in life that are beyond our control. All cause for despair is removed and many cases of mental infirmity and suicide are prevented. With certainty about the future, humanity can be hopeful and patient; without it, it becomes materialistic and egocentric.

The testimony of those who have already lived proves that future happiness is determined by the ethical progress made and the good deeds practiced on Earth. It also proves that future misfortune is the result of present vices and wrongdoings. All who are convinced of that truth, therefore, have a natural tendency to do good and avoid wrongdoing. When the majority of people come to accept that principle and to live accordingly, then goodness will triumph over evilness here on Earth. Human beings will no longer trouble one another. Social institutions will be run for the good of all rather than the profit of a few. In short, mankind will understand that the law of love and charity taught by Christ is the source of happiness, even in this world, and it will base its civil laws upon that ethical law.

The demonstration that the spiritual world exists around us and interacts with the corporeal world reveals to us one of the forces of nature and provides the key to many phenomena in the physical and psychological realm that have been misunderstood until now. When science recognizes this force of nature, it will modify a great many errors that originated when everything was attributed to a single cause—matter. Understanding another cause of nature's phenomena will advance us along the road to progress. It'll be the discovery of an entirely new agent. With the help of the laws identified by the Spiritist Doctrine, the scientific horizon will expand, just as it did with the discovery of the law of gravitation.

When the leading minds of science are willing to make it a subject of study, and proclaim the existence of the spiritual world and its interactions with the physical one, they will infuse the world's youth with the antidote to materialistic ideas and the belief that there is no future. Philosophy, as a discipline, has forever sought to understand the ultimate reality and ascertain the existence of the soul. Isn't it curious that when philosophers are finally able to establish tangible evidence, they deny it, calling it superstition. When a researcher offers a hypothesis about a scientific point, that scientist eagerly looks for and gladly examines everything that may prove the truth of that hypothesis. How, then, can the luminaries of metaphysical philosophy, whose duty it is to establish the truth of the soul, reject the means of obtaining verifiable evidence about its existence?

101. Let's suppose that the spirits aren't able to teach us anything more than we already know or what we're able to learn by ourselves. The proof of the existence of the spiritual world alone incites a change in ideas, and a change in ideas produces a revolution in the order of things. It's this revolution that the Spiritist Doctrine supports and promotes.

102. The spirits, however, do even more than that. Although their communications are sometimes encumbered by difficulties and depend on further validation, when we question enlightened spirits, they can reveal unknown facts to us, explain things we don't understand, and move us more quickly along the path of inner transformation.

Complete, serious study of the Spiritist Doctrine is indispensable in order to claim from it what it can honestly deliver. Staying within its guidelines will prevent deceptions and disappointments.

103. Small causes can bring about great effects: the small seed brings forth an immense tree; the fall of a piece of fruit follows the law that governs the movement of the planets; and frogs jumping in a plate reveal electricity.[39] Similarly, rapping tables proves that the invisible world exists. From that phenomenon, a doctrine was developed that spread around the world in only a few years—a doctrine that regenerates human values by verifying the existence of an afterlife.

104. The Spiritist Doctrine teaches few truths that are completely new. Only eternal truths are absolute. Those taught by the Spiritist Doctrine are founded upon natural laws. The Spiritist Doctrine neither discovered nor invented spirits, nor did it discover the invisible world in which people have always believed. It proves the existence of the spirit world with physical evidence, and presents that world in its true light, disentangling it from dogmatic and superstitious ideas that breed skepticism and unbelief.

The above summary—partial as it may be—should suffice to put on view the foundation upon which the Spiritist Doctrine rests, inform on the essential nature of spirit communication, and highlight the trust that communications deserve.

■ ■ ■

[39] *Translator's Note: By experimenting with frogs in a laboratory, Luigi Galvani (1737–1798) discovered the existence of bioelectric forces in animal tissue.*

CHAPTER III

SOLUTIONS TO SOME PROBLEMS OF PHILOSOPHY

THE PLURALITY OF WORLDS

105. *Is there life on other planets?*

All the spirits have answered this in the affirmative, a conclusion that is also supported by logic. The Earth doesn't occupy a special position in the universe due to its location or its size. There is nothing that would justify Earth's exclusive privilege to harbor life or the belief that God has created millions of planets just for us to look at, especially since most of them are invisible to the naked eye. (See also *The Spirits' Book*, number 55.)

106. *If other worlds are populated, are their inhabitants similar to us in any way? Would they be able to live among us and could we live among them?*

Living organisms must be adapted to the environment in which they live. Fish are adapted to water, birds to the air. If the planetary environments are diverse—as astronomical investigations seem to indicate—then it follows that the organisms inhabiting the various planets must also be different. It's not likely, then, that in their normal state (incarnated in a material body), they could live on other worlds. This is confirmed by information from the higher spirits.

107. *Granted that the worlds are populated, are they on the same level of development as ours, from an intellectual and moral point of view?*

According to the spirits' teachings, the worlds are at very different levels of development. Some are at the same point as ours. Others are more backward; their inhabitants are more crude, more materialistic, more prone to wrongdoing. Still others have beings that are much more advanced morally and intellectually. On those worlds, wrongdoing is unknown, and the arts and sciences have already attained a level of perfection so advanced it's above our comprehension. The physical body is less dense and is immune to suffering, annoyances, and infirmity. There, individuals live in peace and don't seek to harm one another—in short, they are free from the troubles, cares, afflictions, and necessities that affect us on Earth. Finally, there are worlds still more advanced where the body, of almost pure energy, approximates that of the angels. In the developmental ranking of the worlds, ours occupies neither the first nor the last place, but is one of the more materialistic and less developed, morally speaking. (See also *The Gospel - Explained by the Spiritist Doctrine*, Chapter III.)

ABOUT THE SOUL

108. *Where does the soul reside?*

The soul is not, as is generally believed, located in a particular place in the body. It forms a single unity with the perispirit, and integrates with the entire body, which constitutes a complex human being. Death is a natural separation. We can imagine two bodies similar in form, one interpenetrating another, combined during life and separated at death, which destroys one while the other continues to exist.

During life, the soul acts through the vehicles of thought and emotion. It is simultaneously internal and external—that is, it radiates outwardly, being able to separate itself from the body, to transport itself considerable distances, and there to manifest its presence. This is demonstrated objectively by the phenomena produced during hypnotic trances.[40]

109. *Is the soul created at the same time as the body, or prior to it?*

This is one of the most fundamental questions asked because its answer reveals the most important insight, the only one able to explain a multitude of problems that were unsolvable until now. The question is whether the soul did or didn't exist before the body's formation; there can be no middle ground here. If we grant the soul's pre-existence, everything is explained logically and naturally. Not accepting the idea of pre-existence brings up obstacles at every step; even certain dogmas of the Church lose their foundation, which has caused many individuals to become skeptics.

The Spirits have answered the question affirmatively and the facts, as well as logic, leave no doubt in that respect. By accepting the soul's pre-existence, at least as a hypothesis, we can remove most conceptual obstacles.

110. *If the soul existed before its union with the body, did it possess its individuality and consciousness of itself?*

Without individuality and consciousness of itself, it would be as if it didn't exist.

111. *Before its union with the body, had the soul already made some progress, or was it stationary?*

The earlier progress of the soul is demonstrated both by the observation of facts and by the teaching of the spirits.

■ ■ ■

[40] *Translator's Note: Experiments demonstrated that during trance induced by hypnotic means, the subject's consciousness can transport itself to other places and describe the surroundings. The same is true for natural trance. Nowadays, similar results have been observed with a technique called Scientific Remote Viewing, pioneered by Russell Targ and Harold Puthoff at the Stanford Research Institute. Their findings are described in* The Mind Race, *by R. Targ and K. Harary, 1984.*

112. *Did God create souls morally and intellectually equal, or did He make some more virtuous and intelligent than others?*

If God made some more virtuous than others, that preference couldn't be reconciled with Perfect Justice. Since all creatures are God's work, why would God exempt some from effort, while imposing it on others as a condition for them to attain eternal happiness? The inequality of souls in their origin would be the negation of God's justice.

113. *If souls are created equal, how can we explain the diversity of natural aptitudes and predispositions among people on Earth?*

That diversity is the consequence of the progress made by the soul before its union with the body. Souls that are more advanced in intelligence and principles are likely to have lived longer and progressed more before their incarnation.

114. *What is the state of the soul at its origin?*

Souls are created simple and unaware—that is, without knowledge and without cognizance of good and bad—but with equal aptitude for everything. At first, they are in a kind of infancy, without their own will and without complete consciousness of their existence. Little by little, free will develops simultaneously with the intellectual capacity. (See also *The Spirits' Book*, questions 114 to 127.)

115. *Did the soul make its earlier progress in the spirit realm or in a previous corporeal existence?*

In addition to the spirits' teachings about this issue, the different levels of human development—intellectual, moral, and spiritual—on Earth suggests that the earlier progress of the soul must have taken place in a series of corporeal existences. The level of advancement reached may give a rough indication of the number of existences the spirit has had. Proof of this can be found by examining facts that come to our attention daily. (See also *The Spirits' Book*, questions 166 to 222.)

THE EARTHLY JOURNEY

116. *How and at what moment is the soul united with a body?*

From the moment of the physical body's conception, the spirit, although still free (in the spirit realm), is connected by an energy cord to the body with which it will unite. This bond gradually grows stronger as the embryo develops, and the spirit slowly slips into a dazed condition. As birth approaches, the spirit loses consciousness and regains its senses only gradually after the child begins to breathe. Then the union is complete and definitive.

117. *What is the mental state of the soul at the moment of birth?*

Its state is the same as it was before it became united with the body—that is, the soul is in possession of the treasure of ideas and virtues it has acquired over time. Still, because of the disturbance that accompanies its rebirth, its ideas are momentarily in a dormant condition. Their influence in the child's mental life increases in proportion to the brain development.

118. *What is the origin of innate ideas, of precociousness, of great talent for an art or science?*

Innate ideas can have only two sources: the creation of souls better endowed than others, as would be the case if they were created at the same time as the body; or progress made by them prior to incarnation. The first hypothesis is incompatible with the notion of a just God, leaving only the second possibility. Innate ideas are the result of knowledge acquired in previous existences, which serves as a foundation for acquiring new ideas.

119. *How is it possible that people of genius are discovered in classes of society entirely deprived of intellectual culture?*

The fact that they are geniuses proves that innate ideas or abilities are independent of the environment in which the person is born and educated. Environment and education do stimulate ideas, but they can't account for innate knowledge. A person of genius is the incarnation of an advanced spirit that has already progressed considerably. Instruction can make up for a lack in education, but it can't create genius.

120. *Why do we find instinctively good children in perverse surroundings, where they encounter bad examples, and instinctively vicious children in a good environment, where they receive good advice?*

Such tendency is the result of moral progress previously attained, just as innate ideas are the result of intellectual progress.

121. *Why is it that of two sons of the same parents and educated under the same conditions, one is sometimes very smart and the other very slow, one good and the other bad? Why is the child of a genius parent sometimes thickheaded and that of dumb parents, a genius?*

These circumstances support the explanation of the origin of innate ideas. It proves that the soul of a child does not proceed from those of its parents. Otherwise, since the part is of the same nature as the whole, the parents would pass their own qualities and defects on to their children, just as they pass their physical characteristics on to them. Only body proceeds from the body; souls are independent from one another.

122. *If souls are independent from one another, where does the love of parents for their children and that of the children for their parents come from?*

Souls are united by affinity. Birth into a particular family isn't the result of chance, but is often the choice of the spirit to join those it loved in the spiritual world or in its previous existences. On the other hand, parents have the mission of aiding the progress of spirits who incarnate as their children and, to encourage that, God gifted them the power of love. Some, however, fail in their mission and have to carry the responsibility for their actions. (See also *The Spirits' Book*, question 379.)

123. *Why are there bad parents and bad children?*

They are spirits that are bound together in a family not because of affinity, but to serve as mutual instruments of trial, and often, as a corrective for what they did in earlier existences. For instance, a bad child may have been assigned to a parent because that parent also had been a bad child. A bad parent may have been assigned to a child because that child had been an uncaring parent in the past. In this way, they learn their lesson and redeem their wrongs. (*Revue Spirite*, 1861, p. 270.)

124. *Why do some people who are born in humble conditions display traits of dignity and greatness, while others who are born into rich families exhibit only traits of vileness?*

That is an indication of positions previously enjoyed as well as an obvious manifestation of the fundamental character of the spirit.

125. *What is the cause of the unexplained aversion or irresistible (non romantic) attraction, between persons who see each other for the first time?*

Affinities often develop because the persons involved are beings who may have known each other, and perhaps were close to each other, in an earlier existence and who, meeting again in this one, feel a natural sympathy for one another. Instinctive dislikes may also stem from previous relationships.

These two reactions may also have another cause. The spiritual body irradiates its energy around the body, forming a kind of atmosphere imbued with the good or bad qualities of the incarnated spirit. Two persons who meet might experience, through the contact of their energies, an impression that may be agreeable or disagreeable. The fields tend to blend together or to repulse each other according to their similar or dissimilar nature. It's one explanation for the phenomenon of thought transmission as well. Through the contact of their fields, two souls, in some way, read each other's thoughts. They intuit correctly and understand each other without speaking.

126. *Why doesn't humanity remember previous existences? Isn't this memory necessary for future progress?*

See "Forgetfulness of the Past," discussed earlier in this book.

127. *What is the origin of consciousness?*

It is an innate memory of the moral acquisitions made in preceding existences and of the resolutions made by the spirit before incarnating—resolutions that remain outside its conscious awareness during incarnated life.

128. *Do human beings have free will, or are they subject to fate?*

If people's conduct were subject to fate, they would have neither responsibility for the wrong done nor merit for the good they practice. Every punishment would be an injustice, and every reward would be undeserved. Humanity's free will is in accord with God's design. Free will sets human beings apart from other species. In fact, humans' concern for each other is based upon that free will. Anyone who loses that faculty—through an illness, insanity, drunkenness, or idiocy—is separated from society's ordinary functions.

The materialist, who regards all mental faculties as dependent upon the body, reduces humanity to the status of a machine without free will and, consequently, without responsibility for the wrong and merit for the good, practiced.

129. *How can God be the creator of evil?*

God did not create evil. God established laws and these are always good, because God is sovereignly good. Those who observe those laws are perfectly happy. The spirits, however, having free will, don't always observe them, preferring the path of wrongdoing.

130. *Is a human being good or bad at birth?*

It's necessary to make a distinction between the soul and the person. The soul is created simple and unaware—that is, neither good nor bad. It's able, by virtue of its free will, to follow the good or the bad path. In other words, it's able to observe or break God's laws. Whether a person is good or bad is determined by the progress attained by his soul.

131. *What is the origin of good and evil on Earth and why does the latter predominate?*

Wrongdoing on Earth is the result of the imperfection of the spirits incarnated here. Its predominance is an indication of the inferiority of the planet. On more advanced worlds, where only purified spirits incarnate, wrongdoing is rare or doesn't exist at all.

132. *What causes the misfortunes that afflict humanity?*

One world can serve, simultaneously, as both a school for less advanced spirits and a reformatory for guilty spirits. The arduous demands of Earthly life have correlation to the ethical condition of its dwellers. By indulging their vices, they hurt one another and cast around the seeds of their own unhappiness.

133. *Why do we so often see the wrongdoer prosper, while the good struggles?*

To the person who doesn't see beyond the present life and who believes that this life is the only one, this must seem a great injustice. Anyone, who recognizes the plurality of existences and thinks about how brief each of them is compared to eternity, realizes this isn't so. The ill-gotten prosperity of the wrongdoer will have to be accounted for in a future existence. The afflictions of the good, on the other hand, are followed by happiness proportionate to the strength shown in the face of adversity; it will seem like merely one bad day in a long and prosperous existence.

134.   *Why are some people born to poverty and others to opulence? Why are some people blind, deaf, mute, or deformed by incurable diseases, while others possess all their physical faculties? Is it the result of chance or an act of Providence?*

If it were by chance, Providence wouldn't exist. Since we are granting the existence of Providence, however, we must ask how those facts are reconciled with goodness and justice? Many people blame God because they don't understand the cause of such misfortunes. It's easy to comprehend that someone who becomes poor or infirm because of his/her own bad judgment or excesses, suffers through their own failings. However, if the soul is created at the same time as the body, what did it do, either deserve such afflictions or to be exempt from them?

If we acknowledge the justice of God, we cannot fail to see that every effect must have a cause. And if that cause isn't found in the present life, it must be found before it, because in all things, the cause must precede the effect. The presumption, then, is that the soul has already lived, in order to deserve correction or reward.

Spiritist studies reveal to us, in fact, that many people born to misery were rich and esteemed in an earlier existence, in which they badly managed the resources entrusted to them by God. Many who were born to abject poverty were, in a former life, proud and haughty, and abused their power to oppress the weak. These studies often reveal that those who treat others harshly may later have to face similar treatment.

A difficult life, however, doesn't always serve as expiation. Often it's a trial, chosen by a spirit who has the courage and ability to endure it, as a means of advancing more rapidly. Wealth is a trial of much greater danger than misery, because it brings with it temptations and occasions for excesses. Many have shown it to be a trial in which victory is most difficult.

The difference in social status would be the greatest of injustices—when it isn't the consequence of past conduct—if no compensation existed. Humanity may receive the certainty of that truth through the Spiritist Doctrine, which gives people strength to endure life's troubles and accept their lot without envying that of others.

135. *Why are there severely retarded persons?*

If the hypothesis of a single existence were true, the position of the severely retarded would be the least reconcilable with God's justice. No matter how harsh the conditions to which a person is born, he or she is able to improve through education and work. The severely retarded, however, are doomed to suffer prejudice and contempt for their entire earthly lives; for them, escape is impossible. Why, then, were their souls created with such condition?

Spiritist studies about the mentally impaired demonstrate that their spirit is as intelligent as those of other people, and that these afflictions are sometimes experienced by spirits that have greatly abused their intelligence. They suffer severely from their imprisonment in chains they cannot break and from the social stigma they feel their entire lives. Perhaps these same individuals were highly respected in a preceding incarnation.

136. *What is the state of the soul during sleep?*

Only the body reposes during sleep. The soul doesn't sleep. Observations have proven that during sleep the soul has complete liberty and full use of its faculties. The spirit avails itself of the body's rest in order to act separately and go where it wishes. During life, the spirit always remains attached to the body by a subtle energy cord, which serves to call it from any distance whenever its presence becomes necessary to the body. Only at death is that tie broken.

137. *What is the cause of dreams?*

Often, dreams are the result of the spirit's freedom during sleep. Sometimes they are memories of places and persons the spirit has seen or visited during that state. (See also *The Spirits' Book,* question 400 and following; and *The Mediums' Book,* item 284.)

138. *Where do premonitions come from?*

Premonitions are usually vague and intuitive memories of things the spirit learned in its moments of freedom. Sometimes they are hidden warnings given by benevolent spirits.

139. *Why are there both primitive and civilized people on Earth?*

This question is unanswerable without assuming the pre-existence of the soul, unless we admit that God has created primitive souls and civilized souls, which would be the antithesis of Divine Justice. Furthermore, reason refuses to accept that, after death, the primitive should remain in a perpetual state of inferiority, or that the primitive should immediately attain the same elevation as the soul of an enlightened person. Granting that souls originally start from the same point of departure (the only possibility compatible with God's justice), the simultaneous presence of primitive and civilized people on Earth is a fact that confirms that some have made substantial progress while others have barely started the process. With time, then, the primitive soul will arrive at the same level as the enlightened soul; however, each soul can only attain that level by means of successive steps, i.e., incarnations, each more developed and appropriate to its advancement.

140. *Is it possible, as some people think, that the soul only incarnates once and then continues its progress in the spiritual world or on other worlds?*

This idea would be plausible if all peoples of Earth were, strictly speaking, at the same level of development. In that case, one might argue, the Earth would typify a permanent state. Yet, we often see proof to the contrary. If given sufficient time and resources, members of tribal cultures can achieve educational levels on par with individuals born in developed societies. Doesn't this suggest an evolving order and a gradation of personal attainment? And, isn't it consistent with the idea of multiple existences on Earth? If an individual's existence were limited to a single life on Earth, it would be necessary to explain, first, what it is about Earth that gives it a monopoly on the incarnation of spirits, and, second, why such a wide range of differences is found in humankind.

141. *Why do we encounter, in the midst of civilized societies, individuals whose behavior is comparable to the most barbaric savages?*

They are very inferior spirits who come into a more evolved milieu. They are out of place, as a brute would be if suddenly placed in a modern city.

Note: It's not possible, in light of God's goodness and justice, for the soul of a hardened criminal to start the present life from the same point as that of a virtuous man. If we assume that the soul does not exist before the body, then it follows that the soul of the criminal and that of the good person are equally new. For what reason, other than the pre-existence of the soul, is one of them good and the other bad?

142. *Where do the distinctive characters of nations come from?*

A nation consists of spirits who share, more or less, the same tastes and tendencies and who are incarnated in a sympathetic environment that is able to satisfy those inclinations.

143. *How do nations progress and decline?*

If we assume that the soul is created with the body, then the souls of today's humans are as new and primitive as those of the Middle Ages; yet since then, today's nations have developed more refined customs and more advanced knowledge than their precursors. This must be the result of the advancement of the souls involved, for if we assume that, at bodily death, the souls abandon Earth permanently, no progress at all would be made; the improvement of the departing souls would be wasted, since only new souls would arrive daily.

Spirits incarnate in an atmosphere that is sympathetic to, and in relation with, the level of their advancement. For example, an indigenous Asian person, who progressed sufficiently and no longer found in their race an atmosphere corresponding to the level they had attained, would incarnate in a more advanced people. As a generation takes a step forward, by affinity it attracts more advanced spirits who are, perhaps, those who have already lived in the same country and, because of their progress, departed from it once before. It is how, in stages, a nation advances. If most of a nation's new inhabitants were of an inferior nature and its wiser people daily immigrated to other, more advanced countries and never returned, the nation would decline.

Note: These questions provoke others, the answers to which are governed by the same principle. For example, where does the diversity of races on Earth come from? Are some races rebellious to progress? Are certain indigenous races capable of developing to the level of today's advanced societies? Isn't slavery a degradation of life? How can the betterment of the human races be effected? (See also *The Spirits' Book*, question 776 and following.)

HUMAN BEINGS AFTER DEATH

144. *How does the soul separate from the body?*

The disengagement is accomplished gradually. The specific amount of time it takes varies according to the individual and the circumstances of his or her death. The ties that unite the soul to the body are gradually weakened. This process takes place much more slowly when the life was materialistic and sensual. (See also *The Spirits' Book*, question 155.)

145. *What is the soul's situation immediately after the death of the body? Does it instantaneously have self-consciousness? In a word, what does it see? What does it experience?*

At the moment of death, everything appears confused. Some time is needed for the soul to recognize itself. It remains giddy, like a person awakening from a deep sleep who tries to comprehend his surroundings. Lucidity of ideas and memory of the past return as the body's influence dissipates, taking with it the fog that obscured the soul's thoughts.

The period of disorientation following death varies considerably. It may last for only a few hours or for several days, months, or even years. It is shorter for those who, when alive, gave themselves to contemplations about their future state, because they immediately understand their situation. However, it is prolonged in accordance with how materialistic the individual was in life.

The sensation the soul experiences at the moment of death is also variable. The disorientation following death isn't painful to a good person. It's calm and resembles, in every way, the feeling that accompanies a peaceful awakening. However, for the soul with an impure conscience who worshiped the corporeal life at the expense of the spiritual, that moment is full of anxiety, which increases as the soul regains awareness, because it feels fear and a certain terror of what it sees and, especially, of what it imagines.

A sensation akin to physical relief and immense well-being descends upon the soul of the spiritually centered person. Like someone relieved of a burden, the spirit feels happy because it no longer experiences bodily pains that may have tormented it a few moments before. It feels free and unencumbered, like someone relieved of the heavy chains that held them captive. In its new situation, the soul sees and hears all it saw and heard before death, plus other things that escape the perceptions of the bodily organs. It has sensations and perceptions that are unknown to us who are still living. (Mort d'un Spirite, *Revue Spirite*, 1859, p. 244; Le Réveil de l'Esprit, ibid., p. 1862; Obsèques de M. Sanson, ibid., pp. 129 et 171.)

Note: These answers, and all answers regarding the soul's situation during life or after death, are not just an empty theory. They are the result of direct studies made of thousands of individuals observed in all phases and conditions of their spiritual existence, from the lowest to the highest level, accounting for their habits on Earth, type of death, and so forth.

When speaking of the future life, it's often said that no one knows what happens there because no one has come back to tell us about it. This is not true, because it's precisely those who are already there who do come to instruct us about it. God permits this today, more than in any other era, as an additional warning against skepticism and materialism. [41]

146. *Is the soul, upon leaving the body, able to see God?*

Perception depends on one's advancement. The more a spirit advances, the greater its enjoyment of the Divine presence.

147. *If God is everywhere, why aren't all the spirits able to see God?*

God is everywhere, in that God radiates everywhere, so it may be said that the universe is as immersed in the Divinity as we are in solar light. Backward spirits, however, are enveloped in a kind of fog that only dissipates as they illuminate their inner life. Inferior spirits are in relation to God what the incarnate are in relation to the spirits—truly blind.

■ ■ ■

[41] *Translator's Note: The conclusions about the future life maintained by Spiritist literature have been extensively corroborated by modern investigations in the phenomena of clinical death. The fact that they are separated by a century, and have followed two very different approaches to arrive at similar results, is powerful evidence in support of the spirit survival argument. The following are elements most commonly reported in near-death cases: awareness of being dead, awareness of being out of the body, pleasant feelings, travel through a tunnel, communication with a light being, encounter with a deceased relative, and entire life review. Literature and research studies can be accessed at www.iands.org, website of the International Association for Near-Death Studies.*

148. *After death, does the soul have consciousness of its individuality? How do we know it for sure?*

If souls didn't have their individuality after death, this would be, for them as well as for us, the same as if they didn't exist. They wouldn't have any distinctive identity. The criminal would be on the same level as the good person, giving us no incentive to do good.

The soul's individuality is demonstrated in a material manner, so to speak, by the language and qualities displayed by spirits during mediumistic meetings. The various spirits think and act in different manners; some are good and others bad, some wise and others dull, some have strong willpower and others have none. This proves that they are not blended into one homogeneous whole, and that they once animated specific individuals on Earth. Thanks to experimental phenomena, the soul's individuality is no longer a vague theory, but a fact verified through rigorous observation.

The soul recognizes its own individuality because it has its own thoughts and volition. Self-being is further affirmed by the spiritual body, the energy form that shrouds the spirit.

Note: There are those who, in their wish to escape the label of scientific materialists, claim that a universal intelligent principle exists, which we absorb partly at birth and from which we form our souls, and that after death, we return to the common mass and are submerged with others, like drops of water in the ocean. This belief, this notion of transition, shouldn't even be called a form of philosophical spiritualism, since it's as destructive as materialism. The common reservoir of souls would be equivalent to annihilation, considering the loss of individuality.

149. *Does the kind of death influence the soul's state?*

The state of the soul varies considerably, according to the kind of death and, especially, the nature of its habits during life. In the case of natural death, its detachment from the body is accomplished gradually and without shock, beginning even before life is totally extinct. In the case of violent death—by torture, suicide, or accident—the ties are brusquely separated. The spirit, surprised, is stunned by the sudden change and doesn't understand its situation.

A common phenomenon in such cases is that the spirit has the misconception that it's not dead. This illusion may endure many months or even years. In this state, the spirit moves about and is concerned with its earthly affairs as if it were still in the world, and is amazed when it receives no replies to its questions. This isn't limited to cases of violent death; it's also observed in cases in which the individual's life was devoted to worldly passions. (See also *The Spirits' Book,* question 165.)

150. *Where does the soul go after leaving the body?*

It doesn't become lost in the immensity of the infinite, as is generally supposed; rather, it lives in the spirit realms, often amongst those it knew and loved, using its ability to transport itself across great distances instantaneously.

151. *Does the soul retain the love it felt in earthly life?*

It keeps all the higher mental feelings and only sheds those that were physical. Because of this, it's gratified to see relatives and friends, and experiences happiness with their memory.

152. *Does the soul retain the memory of what it did on Earth? Does it still have an interest in the work it didn't complete?*

It depends upon the level of the soul's development and the nature of the work. Advanced spirits are little concerned about worldly matters, of which they are happy to be free. As for the work they began, depending on its importance and usefulness, they sometimes inspire others with the desire to complete it.

153. *Does the soul meet relatives that preceded it in the spirit world?*

Not only does it meet them, but many others as well, particularly the loved ones from other existences. Generally, those who most loved the person come to receive it upon its arrival into the spiritual world and to help free it from earthly ties. However, for a guilty spirit, not seeing its most beloved souls is sometimes a form of expiation.

154. *What, in the spiritual life, is the intellectual and psychological state of the soul of a child who dies in its early years? Does it retain the limitations that it experienced during life?*

The incomplete development of the child's physical organs doesn't permit the spirit the liberty of conscious expression on Earth. Once it's freed from that covering, its faculties are what they were before its incarnation. The spirit, having passed only some instants in life, doesn't retain any of the limitations created by the physical body.

Note: In spirit communications, the spirit of a child may speak as an adult, because it may be an advanced spirit. If sometimes it adopts infantile language, it does so to preserve the delicate and innocent charm that is always attached to the affection of a fragile entity. Incidentally, this explanation also applies to the intellectual state of the soul of the mentally impaired in general, immediately after death.

155. *What difference is there after death between the soul of a wise person and one who is unrefined, or between a primitive and a civilized person?*

The same, essentially, that existed between them during life. Entrance into the spiritual world doesn't endow a person with automatic wisdom. Each soul brings the sum of the knowledge and virtues that it has gained through time.

156. *Do souls progress intellectually after death?*

They progress, more or less, according to their will and some become very advanced; however, they must put into practice in the corporeal life whatever intellectual progress they achieve in the spiritual world. Those who remain stationary repeat an existence similar to the one they left. Those who progress obtain an incarnation of a different order. Because progress is dependent upon the spirit's will, many retain for a long time the tastes, inclinations, and ideas they had during life.

157. *Is a human's destiny in the afterlife irrevocably fixed after death?*

The notion that one's fate in the afterlife is irrevocably sealed is the absolute antithesis of God's justice and goodness, because, in addition to the severely retarded, primitive people, and children who die without fully experiencing life, there are many who are unable to achieve sufficient spiritual progress during earthly existence. Isn't it a demonstration of God's compassion that we are given the allowance and the opportunity to do tomorrow what we were unable to complete today?

If the soul's destiny were irrevocably fixed after death, humans wouldn't die at different ages and God would allow everyone the time necessary to produce the greatest amount of good and to repair the wrong they may have done. Who knows whether the criminal who dies at the age of thirty might have become a good man had he lived to be sixty? If one accepts the notion of Divine Justice, the difference in people's life spans and moral conditions proves the impossibility of the soul's destiny being irrevocably fixed after death.

158. *What, in the future life, is the destiny of children who die in infancy?*

This question is one that best proves the justice and necessity of the plurality of existences. A soul that was incarnated for only a few instants, with no opportunity for doing good or harm, can't earn reward or punishment. According to Christ's teaching everyone is rewarded or punished according to his works, and it's both illogical and contrary to God's justice to believe that, without effort, such a soul is called upon to enjoy, or be deprived of, the blessedness of angels. Nevertheless, that soul must have a logical fate. An intermediate state for all eternity would be equally unjust. An existence interrupted at its beginning can't have any consequence for the soul. The soul's actual destiny will be what it has earned in previous existences, and what it will earn in future existences.

159. *Do souls have occupations in the other life? Do they think about anything besides their joys or sufferings?*

If souls did nothing but think about themselves during eternity, it would be egoism, and God, Who condemns that failing in the corporeal life, would not approve of it in the spiritual life either. Souls, or spirits, have occupations in accordance with their particular levels of advancement. At the same time, they seek to educate and improve themselves. (See also *The Spirits' Book*, question 558.)

160. *What sufferings do souls experience after death? Are sinful souls tortured in flames?*

Today,[42] the Church recognizes perfectly well that the fire of hell is entirely symbolic and not physical; however, it doesn't define the actual nature of the sufferings. Mediumistic communications, on the other hand, present those sufferings to us; we are able to understand them and be convinced that, despite not being the result of actual fires which could not effectively burn immaterial souls, they are no less poignant in certain cases.

Furthermore, those sufferings are not uniform. They vary according to the nature and level of the wrong committed. Those same wrongs are almost always the instruments of punishment. Thus, assassins are mesmerized by the location of their crime and the incessant contempla-

■■■

[42] *Translator's Note: The author refers to the time when Spiritist literature was first introduced—late 1850s.*

tion of their victims. The corrective action for those devoted to the lusts of the flesh is that they retain those desires along with an inability to satisfy them, which, for them, is sheer torture. Certain avaricious souls are bound to continue suffering the anxieties they endured during life because of their greed; others keep constant watch over their treasures, in perpetual anguish of being robbed. In short, there is no defect, moral flaw, or harmful act that doesn't have its natural consequence and correction in the spiritual world. Therefore, there's no need for a specific physical place called hell. Wherever a perverse spirit is, hell will be within it.

In addition to the sufferings in the spirit realm, the soul may have to continue its trials and corrections in a new incarnation, where it often experiences the harm it caused others to suffer: humiliation, if it were haughty; poverty, if avaricious; difficult children, if a bad child, etc. As we have said, Earth resembles, in some ways, a rehabilitation center—a place from which each spirit is able to gain release by improving itself enough to earn a happier existence. (See also *The Spirits' Book,* question 237, and Chapter 28.)

161. *Is prayer useful to suffering souls?*

All good spirits recommend prayer, and troubled spirits request it as a means of alleviating their sufferings. The soul for which it's offered feels comforted because it recognizes in prayer a testimony of affection. The unhappy are always consoled when they find someone who empathizes with their sorrows. At the same time, prayer encourages the spirit to admit to, and feel sorry for, its misdeeds, and fosters the desire to do what is necessary to attain a happier condition. It's in this sense that prayer can alleviate a soul's sufferings. (See also *The Spirits' Book,* question 664.)

162. *What joys do blessed souls experience? Do they spend eternity in contemplation?*

Justice dictates that reward must be in proportion to merit, just as the corrective should suit the gravity of the crime. There are, then, infinite levels in the joys of the soul from the instant it enters upon the path of good until it attains the higher states of illumination. The happiness of good spirits consists of having a broad range of knowledge and in not feeling hate, jealousy, envy, ambition, or any of the passions that degrade humanity. The love that unites good spirits is the source of their supreme happiness. They don't experience the needs, sufferings, or anxieties of material life.

A state of perpetual contemplation, on the other hand, would be a boring happiness. It would be the fate of the egoist—an interminably useless existence. Spiritual life is, on the contrary, full of incessant activity. As God's agents in the functioning of the universe, spirits receive missions proportionate to their advancement. Accomplishing these missions make the spirits happy because they furnish them with opportunities to serve and do good. (See also *The Spirits' Book,* question 558.)

We conclude this brief review of the Spiritist Doctrine by leaving an open invitation to those who oppose the idea of reincarnation and reject the principles of the Spiritist Doctrine to offer a more logical solution to so many existential questions.

SPIRITISM
IN ITS SIMPLEST
EXPRESSION

SPIRITISM
IN ITS SIMPLEST EXPRESSION

Historical SYNOPSIS

In 1848, reports of a series of strange phenomena—noises, rapping, moving objects—that had no known cause, received attention in the United States. These phenomena often occurred spontaneously, with unusual intensity and persistence. It was also observed that they often took place in the presence of certain individuals called "mediums," who could cause them at will, making it possible to repeat these experiences. Tables were usually used in these sessions because they were easy to move and easier for participants to sit around than any other piece of furniture. Thus, table turning was first observed, followed by its movement in all directions, as well as shaking, railing, soaring, violent rapping, and so forth. The phenomenon was referred to initially as "table-turning" or "rapping tables."

At first, the explanation that the phenomena were the result of an electric or magnetic current or the action of some unknown form of energy seemed satisfactory. However, intelligent outcomes were evident in these phenomena, suggesting that the phenomena obeyed the will of some intelligent agent. On command, tables moved right or left, toward the person indicated, stood on one or two legs, rapped a requested number of times, or kept a rhythm. It became rapidly apparent that the cause could not be purely physical. According to the axiom, "If every effect has a cause, an intelligent effect must have an intelligent cause," it was concluded that the source of these phenomena had to be some intelligent cause.

What was the nature of this force? It was first thought that it could be a reflection of the medium's or the participants' intelligence, but experience soon proved that impossible. Some of the results obtained were totally different from the thought perspective and knowledge of those present and even contradictory to their beliefs, their wills, or their wishes. Therefore, the phenomena could only be due to some yet unknown entity. Proof was simple to obtain. Conversations were started with various entities by assigning an arbitrary number of raps to yes and to no or to each letter of the alphabet. In this manner, questions were asked and answered. This phenomenon became known as the "talking tables." When the entities were asked about their nature, they responded that they were spirits; individualities who belonged to the invisible realm. Since the same results were obtained at many different locations by different individuals, and were observed by people of high intellectual standing and credibility, it was simply not possible for all of them to be suffering from an illusion.

From the United States, the phenomena spread to France and the rest of Europe, where, for several years, rapping tables became fashionable and even a salon entertainment. Subsequently, people tired of them and pursued other distractions.

It was not long before the phenomena reappeared under another guise, which raised it to more than a simple pastime. The sheer number of incidents makes it impossible to report here on the complete scope of this resurgence.

Before examining the usual characteristics of the phenomena, it is important to note that many critics questioned their authenticity. Some, disregarding the investigators' independence and reputations, claimed the phenomena were merely illusion, clever slights-of-hand. Materialists—those who will admit to nothing but the material world, who believe only in visible, tangible things and that everything ends with the body's demise, and who consider themselves strong minds—rejected the notion of invisible spirits, considering them absurd fantasy. They ridiculed those who took the matter as worthy of consideration, calling them lunatics.

Others, unable to deny the facts but locked into their religious dogmas, attributed the phenomena to the devil and, on that basis, attempted to scare the fainthearted. However, fear of the devil was losing its grip on the human mind. The devil has been talked about so much, painted in so many different ways, that everyone is familiar with the concept. In fact, many people decided to make the best of the opportunity to examine the facts. So the warnings actually served as advertisements. Thus, except for a small number of the skittish, the news of the supposed appearance of the devil was, to some extent, exciting for those who had seen his similitude only in paintings or on the stage. Therefore, those who intended to prevent the spread of the new ideas ended up as their unwitting advertising agents.

Other critics were no more successful, since they had only their personal opinions with which to challenge well-established facts. In fact, the published writings of these critics show a complete disregard for the facts. Nowhere in these writings is there a peremptory demonstration of the impossibility of the phenomena. Their entire argument can be summed up in the sentiment, "I do not believe in it, therefore it does not exist. All those who do believe in it are foolish. We know better, as this is a matter of pure reason and common sense." Both the serious and the joker supported their arguments only with personal opinions, empty of any proof. The critics' outcry was not disastrous, however, as untold numbers of people have embraced the cause.

Rapping, the initial means of communication, was slow and inadequate. It then became clear that, by affixing a pencil to some light object—a basket, a small board, or anything else which the medium's fingers could lightly touch—the object could move from letter to letter. Later, it was discovered that such objects could be dispensed with altogether—experience showed that the spirit who acts on an inert body, controlling it at will, could just as easily act on an arm or a hand to move the pencil. Thus, the writing mediums emerged, i.e., people who write not of their own accord, but under the direction of spirits, whose instruments or interpreters they become. From then on, there were no more constraints to communication, and the exchange of ideas proceeded with the same spontaneity as it does among the living, opening up a vast field for exploration. Communication with the spirits enabled humanity to discover an entirely new world—the unseen (spiritual) world—just as the microscope enabled the discovery of the world of the infinitely small.

What are these spirits? What is their role in the Universe? Why do they communicate with us mortals? These were the first questions requiring an answer. The spirits soon revealed that they are not a separate class of beings in creation, but the souls of those who had lived on Earth or on other worlds, and that once freed of their material shells—their bodies—these souls can and do move freely through space. It was no longer possible to doubt this fact, once the spirits of participants' deceased relatives and friends appeared among those who could converse, proving that they still exist, that death comes only to the body, while the soul, or spirit, lives forever. They attested to the fact that they may come close to us, and are able to see us as they did when their bodies were alive, and that they still care for those whom they loved, those whose memory was sweet to them.

Overall, people have a mistaken notion of the spirits. Spirits are not, as many think, abstract, vague, indefinite beings, nor are they anything resembling luminosity or spark. Quite the contrary, they are very real beings, with clear identities and shapes. Through the following explanation, we can have an approximate idea of them:

> A human being comprises three essential parts: the *soul*, or *spirit*, which is the intelligent element, the site of thought, will, and moral sense; the body, the material shell, which is heavy and coarse and functions as a link between the spirit and the physical world around it; and the *perispirit*, (or spiritual body) which is a light, energy shell, an intermediary and a bond connecting the spirit to the body. When the outer shell becomes worn out by use and can no longer perform its functions, it dies and the spirit sheds it, just as a snake sheds its skin or a tree its bark. In other words, just as one discards old clothes that

are no longer useful, the spirit discards its body. This is what we call death. Thus, death is no more than the abandonment of the spirit's coarse shell; only the body dies.

In a way, during life, the spirit is limited by the material body. The body's demise frees the spirit from those bonds. The spirit lets go of the body and gains its freedom, like a butterfly abandons its chrysalis. Only the physical body is left behind; the perispirit is retained, forming a sort of ethereal body, vaporous and intangible to us, but usually in human form. In its normal state, the perispirit is invisible, but the spirit can modify it so that, like a condensing vapor, it becomes temporarily visible to our eyes and even palpable, thus explaining the apparitions we sometimes see. It is through the perispirit that the spirit is able to interact with matter to produce phenomena such as noises, movements of objects, and writing.[43]

Rapping and moving objects are ways certain spirits make their presence known, just as a person knocks on a door to make his arrival known. Some don't limit themselves to moderate noises, but produce the louder sounds of breaking dishes, slamming doors, or moving furniture.[44]

While they are able to express their thoughts by means of raps or other agreed upon movements, writing and oral communications offer more efficient, faster, and comfortable means of communication, and are preferred. Furthermore, just as spirits can cause letters to be written, they can easily control the hand to paint, draw, write music, or perform on some instrument. In other words, lacking a body of their own, they can use

■■■

[43] Translator's Note: The phenomenon was extensively documented by Sir William Crookes in the United Kingdom in the 1870s who, for over ten years, conducted experiments with the spirit Katie King. His published research papers were collected and published in Crookes and the Spirit World, 1971. Similar phenomena have been widely documented in the history of the Catholic Church, see http://www.catholicdoors.com/isit/approved.htm

■■■

[44] Translator's Note: Although these are technically possible, they have fallen in the category of hauntings, a kind of phenomena that has no ethical or intellectual value. They have value only as evidence of a supernatural realm or mechanism.

the arms of a willing intermediary—a medium—to manifest themselves in a tangible manner.

Spirits can also communicate visually or aurally. Certain persons, known as "seeing mediums," can see them. Others, considered "auditive mediums," are able to hear the spirits and converse with them. Spirits presenting themselves visually usually appear as they looked when alive on Earth, only more vaporous. On some occasions, their appearance may so closely resemble that of a living person that the illusion is perfect and they are taken for flesh-and-blood people, able to shake hands, and if it were not for their sudden disappearance, would never be suspected of being spirits.

A permanent and generalized ability to see spirits is very rare, but occasional visions are fairly frequent, especially immediately after the person's bodily death. The individual who has just passed is sometimes anxious to see relatives and friends, as if wanting to tell them that they have passed on and show that they continue to live.

Anyone can search his or her memory and recall visions of this kind, which, at the time, did not seem particularly important. These appearances occur not only at night, during sleep, but also in broad daylight. Such facts were once considered supernatural and attributed to sorcery. Today, the skeptics attribute them to the imagination. But now that Spiritist research has provided the key, it is understood how these phenomena occur and that they are completely natural.

There are those who think that spirits, just because they are spirits, must have absolute knowledge and wisdom. This is a mistake, as experience reveals. Among the communications received from spirits, there are some that are truly sublime in their depth, their eloquence, and their wisdom and principles; they reflect only goodness and benevolence. But there are also many others that are vulgar, frivolous, trivial, and even rude, in which the spirits show the most perverse instincts. It is obvious, then, that they can't possibly come from the same spirit source; hence, if there are good spirits, there are also coarse ones. Since the spirits are no more than the souls of women and men, they clearly cannot become virtuous merely by leaving their bodies.

They retain the flawed principles and views that represent their present level of progress that they displayed during life. Therefore, all degrees of goodness and badness, knowledge and ignorance, can be found among the spirits.

In general, spirits appreciate the opportunity to communicate. It is a satisfaction for them to know they are not forgotten. They are eager to describe their impressions on leaving life on Earth, their new condition, and the nature of their joys and struggles in the realm in which they live. Some are very happy; others seem disheartened. Some even suffer indescribable torments.

It became possible, then, to study them in almost every phase of their new lives. Further, this knowledge was correlated with information about their character and habits while alive, the kind of life they led, and the good or bad use they made of their earthly lives. By systematically questioning them, cataloging and comparing their answers, some reasonably accurate images started to surface. These images support important inferences about what our lives in the next realm will be like, of the happy or unhappy destinies awaiting us there.

The instructions provided by enlightened spirits regarding these matters, of so much interest to humanity, and their answers to the questions we submitted to them, were gathered and carefully coordinated. They constitute a complete science, an ethical and philosophical system called Spiritism (also known as Christian Spiritism). Thus, Spiritism is the doctrine based on the existence, manifestations, and teachings of the spirits. This doctrine is fully presented, in its philosophical sense, in *The Spirits' Book*; in its practical and experimental aspects in *The Mediums' Book*; and in its ethical ramifications in *The Gospel—Explained by the Spiritist Doctrine*. The following analysis evaluates the variety, scope, and importance of the subjects covered in these works.

As previously mentioned, the starting point of Spiritism was the ordinary phenomenon of table-turning, which appealed more to curiosity than to the intelligence. Once that curiosity was satisfied, participants lost interest because they didn't understand the cause of what they saw. But once a theory to explain the phenomenon was put forth, interest was rekindled, especially when it became known that those rapping tables that had briefly amused so many were actually the source of an ethical doctrine concerning the soul—a doctrine that soothed the anxiety of existential doubt and satisfied all those aspirations that had been frustrated by our incomplete knowledge about humanity's future. Thoughtful people regarded the new doctrine as a boon, and since then, the number of its adherents has grown unbelievably fast. In the span of a few years, it gathered many followers all over the world, especially among educated people, at an ever-increasing pace. Today it can be said that the Spiritist Doctrine has earned its place among the world philosophies. It rests on bases that defy the efforts of adversaries who are intent on fighting it; all their attacks and criticism have not slowed down its march at all. This is a fact that opponents struggle to accept. The spirits simply say that if the number of followers is growing, it's because they find the Doctrine's logic sounder and prefer it over the critics' arguments.

Yet ideas advanced by the Spiritist Doctrine aren't really a modern discovery. The facts and principles on which it is based can be found in the beginnings of time. There are traces of it in the beliefs of all peoples, in all religions, and in ancient writings. The facts were merely never fully studied before and were often interpreted in the context of superstitious ideas. Since spirits are no more than the souls of men and women, spirits have existed ever since there were men and women. Spiritism neither invented nor even discovered them. Spirits, or souls, are able to communicate with the living because a law of nature enables them to do so; consequently, they were always able to do so. We have always and everywhere found evidence of such manifestations, particularly in biblical accounts.

What is modern is the logical explanation of the facts, the more precise knowledge of the nature of the spirits, their role and their mode of action, and the revelations regarding our future—in other words, the transformation of the subject into a field of scientific study and an ethical philosophy. The ancients knew the principle, and in modern times we study their processes. In antiquity, the study of these phenomena was a privilege reserved to religious casts, who revealed them only to those initiated into their mysteries. During the Middle Ages, those who dealt with these matters were considered witches and were burned at the stake. Today, there is no mystery for anyone and nobody is burned alive. Everything is done publicly, and since people with the appropriate gifts are found everywhere, anyone can conduct their own inquiry or seek knowledge in one's own way.

Even the doctrine taught today by the spirits is not new. Fragments of it are found among most of the philosophies of India, Egypt, and Greece, and it is complete in Jesus' teachings. So what is Spiritism all about? It brings reconfirmation with new testimonies, demonstrating, through facts, those truths that were unknown, and restoring those truths that were misunderstood to their true sense.

It's true that the Spiritist Doctrine teaches nothing new. Still, isn't it worthwhile to prove, beyond doubt, the soul's existence, its survival of the body, its individuality after death, its immortality, and even future punishments and rewards? How many people believe in these things, yet hide a vague feeling of doubt, wondering to themselves, "What if it isn't true?" How many became disbelievers simply because their reason couldn't accept the future that religion had shown to them? Isn't it important for the faltering believer to be able to say to himself, "Now I am certain!" Using facts and pure logic, Christian Spiritism dispels the anxiety of doubt and returns those who have strayed to the path of faith. By revealing the existence of the invisible world surrounding us, of which we were previously unaware, the Spiritist Doctrine lets us learn the conditions for our future happiness or unhappiness from those who have lived before; it explains the reason for our suffering in this world and shows us the means to soften that pain.

The inevitable consequence of the acceptance of the Spiritist Doctrine will be the decline of scientific materialism on the strength of the evidence. Human beings will rise above earthly anxieties. The notion of a fragile and short earthly existence will give way to the awesome reality of future life and eternity. Knowing the cause and the purpose of their trials, people undergo them with strength and courage, because they know that through them, they will attain a better position. The examples of those who return from the next realm to describe their joys and pains demonstrates the reality of the future life, and also demonstrates that Divine Justice allows no wrong to go uncorrected and no virtue to go unrewarded. The communications from the loved ones we've lost, which bring us so much comfort, give us testimony not only of their continued existence, but also of the fact that they are no farther from us than if they were living in another country.

The Spiritist Doctrine softens the bitterness of life's disappointments, calms the soul's desperation and agitations, dispels the doubts and fears related to the future life, and removes any inclinations to shorten life through suicide. It brings happiness to those who delve deeply into it, and that is the reason for its rapid spread.

From the religious point of view, the Spiritist Doctrine is based on the fundamental tenets of all religions: God, the soul, immortality, and future rewards. It is free, however, of any rituals, liturgies, and sacraments. Similar to all religions, its objective is to show to those who deny or doubt it, that the soul does exist and that it survives the body and, after death, experiences the consequences of good or wrong deeds.

The belief in the survival of the soul is found in all religions and cultures. Their manifestations have occurred throughout time, and all religions, without exception, have stories on this subject. Catholics, Orthodox Christians, Protestants, Jews, and Muslims can all believe in the existence of spirits, and accept the essential tenets of the Spiritist Doctrine without giving up their religious beliefs. The proof of this is that the Spiritist movement has members from all religious denominations.

As an ethical philosophy, the Spiritist Doctrine is essentially Christian. Its chief aspiration is the development and application of Christian morality, the purest of all, the superiority of which no one doubts. Its ethical philosophy is for everyone's use.

Independent as it is of any particular religious denomination, the Spiritist Doctrine does not favor one over another nor concern itself with their particular dogmas. Neither does it constitute a formal religion; it has neither priests nor temples. In answer to the question of whether one should follow one practice or another, its only response is: "Do what your conscience dictates. God always considers the intention." In other words, the Spiritist Doctrine imposes nothing on anyone. It does not address itself to those who have faith and to whom such faith is sufficient, but rather to the large class of people insecure in their faith and to the unbelievers. It does not try to separate anybody from their churches. In fact, the Spiritist Doctrine helps them to return to their faith; it is up to the churches to do the rest.

It's true that the Spiritist Doctrine combats ideas such as the eternity of punishment, the fires of hell, and the personification of the devil. Yet, isn't it true that those ideas have always stimulated disbelief and continue to do so even today? If by substituting these dogmas with a rational explanation, the Spiritist Doctrine can restore faith to those who have lost it, isn't it rendering a service to religion? A venerable man of the Church said in this regard, "The Doctrine makes one to believe in something; faith in something is always better than to have no faith at all."

Since spirit and soul are essentially the same, one cannot deny the existence of spirits without denying the existence of the soul. Once this existence is accepted, the question is reduced to its simplest expression, "Can the souls of those who passed on communicate with those who live?" The Spiritist Doctrine provides tangible proof that the answer must be in the affirmative; what proof has been offered that it is NOT possible? And if it's possible, then all the denials in the world will not make it any less so; such communication is not a theory or a system, but a law of nature. All that a person can do is to learn to accept this reality and revise his or her beliefs and behavior accordingly.

SUMMARY OF PRINCIPLES

1.   God is the supreme intelligence, the primary cause of all things. God is eternal, unique, immaterial, immutable, omnipotent, supremely just and good. God is infinite in all attributes; if imperfect in even one attribute, God would not be God.

2.   God created the matter that forms the worlds. God also created intelligent beings, which we call spirits, who are active in the functioning of the material worlds according to the laws of creation. Because of their nature, these beings are capable of perfectibility; as they become more perfect, they more closely approach the Divinity.

3.   The spirit itself is the intelligent principle. We don't know its intimate nature. To us, it is non material, since it in no way resembles physical matter as we know it.

4.   Spirits are individual beings. They have a subtle, ethereal, nearly massless covering we call the perispirit, a kind of energy body that serves as a blueprint for the human form. Spirits populate space, through which they move. They make up the unseen world.

5.   We don't know the origin or the manner of the spirits' creation. We know only that they were created simple and unaware, i.e., without knowledge or awareness of right and wrong, but with equal capacity for everything, since God, as a principle of justice, would not exempt them from the work necessary for their progress. In their early states, spirits have neither a will of their own nor a clear awareness of their own selfhood.

6.   As free will and self-awareness develop, the spirit fulfills God's design, expressed in the following affirmation "You can aspire to supreme happiness after acquiring knowledge and performing the tasks assigned to you. Thus, go and work to make progress. That is the objective. You shall attain perfection by honoring the laws I have engraved in your conscience."

As a result of their free will, some take the shorter road—that of goodness—and others the longer one—that of wrongdoing.

7. God did not create evil. God instituted laws. Those who follow these laws will attain happiness. But spirits, using free will, didn't always follow them, and impiety was a consequence of their disregard for the law. Thus, we can say that good is everything that conforms to God's law, and evil is everything that goes against that law.

8. To contribute to the tasks of the material worlds as agents of the Divine, spirits temporarily adopt a physical body. By means of the efforts necessary to maintain the body, they improve their intelligence, and by practicing God's law, they acquire the qualities that earn them happiness.

9. Incarnation is not punishment. It is necessary for the spirit's development and to the fulfillment of the Divine Design. Everyone must experience it, whether they choose the path of good or of wrongdoing. But those who choose the path of good attain perfection earlier. They achieve it with less suffering.

10. While incarnated on earth, spirits constitute humanity. The spirits are not circumscribed to Earth, but also populate other realms in space.

11. The spirit is called "soul" while incarnated in a physical body. The animal world helps human beings to accomplish their fundamental task. The nature and intelligence of animals is in accord with their roles.

12. The spirit's betterment is the fruit of its own efforts. Since it's impossible to acquire all the intellectual and moral qualities necessary to reach its goal in a single physical lifetime, the spirit accomplishes it through a series of existences, and during each one, it progresses a few steps along the road to perfection.

13. During each physical existence, the spirit performs a set of tasks in conformance with its progress. The harder and more difficult the tasks, the greater is the merit of its accomplishment. Thus, each incarnation is a step in the ladder of progress. Each task fulfilled brings the spirit closer to its goal. The number of incarnations is indeterminate. The strength of will, and effort toward moral betterment, affect the number of incarnations, just as a worker's will determines whether a job is completed in a longer or shorter time.

14. When an incarnation is misused, it does not benefit the spirit, who will have to start over under more or less arduous conditions. We see this process in everyday life when we are forced to do tomorrow what we didn't do today, or when we have to redo a job poorly done.

15. The spiritual life is a spirit's normal life. Physical life is transitory, temporary, and no more than an instant in eternity.

16. During the intervals between physical existences, the spirit is free. There is no fixed duration to this freedom. In this state, the spirit can be either happy or unhappy, depending on how much it profited from its last incarnation. Between lives, it studies the factors that affected its progress, makes new resolutions, and plans the trials best suited to its progress. Though it hopes to really act on these resolutions, the spirit may fail to keep them when incarnated.

17. The spirit who is laden with guilt, experiences inner anguish in the spirit world and both physical and psychological torment while incarnated. Its afflictions are a consequence of its failings, i.e., its infringements of God's law. Thus, suffering is, simultaneously, atonement for the past and a test of strength for the future. In this manner, one who was prideful may take on a new life in humbling circumstances; a cruel leader, one of servitude; a miser, a life of necessity.

18. The worlds are suited to the progress of spirits. The conditions of life on these worlds vary widely. The less advanced the spirit, the heavier and coarser the body it utilizes. As a spirit becomes more purified, it advances to worlds that are morally and physically superior. Earth is neither the highest nor the lowest of these worlds, but it is still of a somewhat lower condition.

19. Spirits that incurred serious guilt, incarnate in less-advanced worlds, where they atone for their wrongs through arduous life situations. For them, these worlds are, so to speak, a purgatory. Their efforts toward interior transformation determine whether, and when, they leave for better circumstances. For many spirits, Earth is one of these worlds.

20. Since God is supremely just and good, nobody is condemned to perpetual punishment for temporary sins. God offers everyone the means to moral progress and to repair wrong they may have done. God forgives, but expects a change of ways, reparations, and a return to good. Therefore, the duration of a corrective experience depends on the spirit's persistence in wrongdoing. Consequently, suffering is eternal only for those who eternally persist in doing wrong. Still, as soon as any sign of repentance is observed, God showers the individual with mercy. We must, therefore, understand that the eternity of sufferings is a relative notion and must not be taken in the absolute sense.

21. When spirits incarnate, they bring with them the sum of what they have acquired during previous existences. It's for this reason that individuals show certain innate abilities, or certain good or bad tendencies. Bad tendencies are the remainders of imperfections the spirit hasn't yet been able to completely overcome. They offer a glimpse of the errors that marked the spirit's past. Figuratively speaking, they are the real original sins, i.e., the flaws inherent to the individual's nature. During each existence, the spirit must work to eliminate some of these imperfections.

22.   Forgetfulness of previous existences is one of God's bless-
ings. It saves people from memories that can often be
painful. In each new existence, a person is what she or he
determines. Each life is a new starting point. They recognize only their current imperfections. They know that
most imperfections are moral in essence and offer clues of
the wrongs committed. If, in previous incarnations, a person had defects that they no longer have, they needn't
worry about them in the current life. They can focus on
only those that remain.

23.   If we accept that the soul did not live previously, we also
have to accept that it was created at the same time as the
body. If we accept this, then a soul would have no relation
to others preceding it. One wonders why God, Who is
supremely just and good, would hold an innocent soul
responsible for sins committed by the father of the human
race (Adam), blaming it for an original sin that it did not
commit. If, instead, we accept the view that the reborn
soul brings the seed of the imperfections from previous
existences, that in the current existence it suffers the consequences of past deeds, then we are providing a logical
explanation for the biblically based notion of original sin.
Such an explanation is one that everyone can understand
and accept, because the soul is then held responsible only
for its own actions.

24.   The diversity in innate moral and intellectual abilities is
proof that the soul has lived before. If it had been created
at the same time as its current body, this would mean God
created some souls more advanced than others, which is
contrary to the goodness of God. Why are there savages
and civilized people, good and bad persons, intelligent
and witless individuals? This is all readily explained if we
accept that some have lived longer than others and
acquired more skills.

25.   If the current existence were the only one, and if it alone
determined the soul's future for all eternity, then what
would be the fate of children who die in infancy? Since

they practiced neither good nor wrong, they deserve neither reward nor punishment. According to Christ's
words, since each of us is rewarded or punished according to our own actions, such children are not entitled to
the perfect happiness of the angels, but neither should
they be deprived of it. Suffice it to say that in another
incarnation, they will be able to do what they couldn't do
in their short existence.

26. Similarly, what should the fate be of the mentally
impaired? Having no awareness of good and bad, right
and wrong, they are not responsible for their actions.
Could God be considered just and good if God had created such souls, destined to a miserable existence without
compensation? However, if we accept that the soul of the
mentally impaired is enduring the consequences of its
own transgressions in a body unable to express its
thoughts, then the existence of such a person is not
incompatible with God's justice.

27. During its successive incarnations, the spirit gradually
rids itself of its imperfections, and, having improved itself
through its own effort, eventually attains a state where
physical existences are no longer necessary. It then attains
the state of pure spirit, or angelical being, simultaneously
enjoying a purely spiritual life and untainted happiness.

28. Since women and men are on Earth for the purpose of
purification, God—like any good parent—does not leave
them there to fend for themselves without guidance.
Individuals have their spiritual guides, or guardian
angels, who look out for them and try to lead them onto
the right path. There are also enlightened spirits who
incarnate from time to time to enlighten humanity by
means of their achievements and to help it advance. In
addition to having engraved the Law in everyone's conscience, God also articulated it explicitly. First, God sent
Moses. But Moses' laws were suitable only to the people
of his time. Moses' teachings emphasized life on Earth
and temporal punishments and rewards. Then came

Christ, who completed Moses' law with higher level
teachings: plurality of existences,[45] spiritual life, moral
pains and rewards. Moses guided people through fear,
Christ through love and charity.[46]

29.   The Spiritist Doctrine combines theory and evidence. It
shows the future of the soul through the presentation of
unimpeachable facts. It says clearly and without equivo-
cation what Christ conveyed through parables. It
explains unknown truths and those that were misinter-
preted. It reveals the existence of the invisible, or spirit,
world and initiates humanity into the mysteries of the
future life. It opposes (scientific) materialism, which is a

■ ■ ■

[45] *Translator's Note: Matthew, 17:10–12 ("The disciples asked him, 'Why then do the
teachers of the law say that Elijah must come first?' Jesus replied, 'To be sure, Elijah
comes and will restore all things. But I tell you, Elijah has already come, and they did not
recognize him, but have done to him everything they wished. In the same way the Son of
Man is going to suffer at their hands.' Then the disciples understood that he was talking
to them about John the Baptist."), and John, 3:1-2 ("Now there was a man of the
Pharisees named Nicodemus, a member of the Jewish ruling council. He came to Jesus at
night and said, 'Rabbi, we know you are a teacher who has come from God. For no one
could perform the miraculous signs you are doing if God were not with him.' In reply
Jesus declared, 'I tell you the truth, no one can see the kingdom of God unless he is born
again.' 'How can a man be born when he is old?' Nicodemus asked. 'Surely, he cannot
enter a second time into his mother's womb to be born!' Jesus answered, 'I tell you the
truth, no one can enter the kingdom of God unless he is born of water and the Spirit.
Flesh gives birth to flesh, but the Spirit gives birth to spirit. You should not be surprised
at my saying, You must be born again.'")*

■ ■ ■

[46] *Translator's Note: The word in the French original is* charité, *which is explicitly
characterized by Allan Kardec as charity in its most inclusive meaning. Throughout
the book, the word* charité *is employed to express Christian love in its purest reflection
of the Greek word* agape. *In the English language, and particularly in religious usage,
the word 'love' has been substituted in all instances in the Revised Version of the New
Testament (published in 1811). Confirmation of this usage appears in the translation of
Paul's words, "If I speak in the tongues of men and of angels, but have no love…" [1
Corinthians 13:2] which, in romance languages might correspond to charity. For con-
sistency, when the original French employed the word* charité *it has been translated as
love, except in the few circumstances where the meaning was "acts or works of charity
to the poor." This decision is also motivated by the fact that the predominant meaning
of the word charity in the United States is: (a) actions for the needy, or (b) charitable
institution. The Oxford English Dictionary and Le Petit Robert Dictionnaire de la
Langue Française were followed in the determination of the best use and meaning for
each occurence.*

rebellion against God's power. It has come, finally, to help establish among humanity the kingdom of love and solidarity announced by Christ. Moses prepared the ground, Christ seeded it, and the Spiritist Doctrine comes to help in the harvest.

30. The Spiritist Doctrine is not so much a new light as a broader one, since it is appearing all over the world, thanks to those who lived before. By making evident what was obscure, it puts an end to erroneous interpretations. It is intended to unite all of mankind in a single belief in only one God and on the universality of Divine Law. Finally, it proclaims the arrival of the times announced by Christ and the prophets.

31. The misfortunes that befall humanity on Earth have their origins in pride, selfishness, and all base passions. Because of these moral weaknesses, human beings turn angry and indifferent with one another, and act in ways that hurt each other. As soon as love (charity) and humbleness replace selfishness and pride, people will cease to harm each other. Each one will respect the other's rights, resulting in harmony and justice among all people.

32. But how can the selfishness and pride that seem inherent in the human heart be destroyed? Selfishness and pride are found in the hearts of women and men because they are spirits who, having trod the pathways of wrong, were assigned to Earth to work on their moral imperfections. They are still trying to change the nature of the seeds planted in prior lives. The Spiritist Doctrine is another invitation for humanity to practice Christ's law of love and charity.

33. Since Earth is entering the stage in which spiritual fulfillment and peace should be foremost, Providence does not want wrongdoing spirits to continue to delay Earth's transformation. Therefore, they will have to leave Earth. They will have to deal with their inclinations on less advanced worlds, where, once again, they will work for their own betterment through a series of existences, certainly less pleasing and more trying than those they lived on Earth.

On such worlds they will form new, more enlightened groups, to further the progress of the local inhabitants. The knowledge they have acquired becomes then an instrument of progress. They will leave those worlds for better ones only after they have progressed enough, and so it will be, until they attain the pure state. If, so to speak, Earth felt like purgatory for them, the less-advanced realms to which they are sent will resemble the earthly descriptions of hell, except that, even in those worlds, hope for a better life is never in vain.

34. At the same time, as the banned spirits move out of Earth, others will come to join the Earth community. Their moral values will be higher, and largely in agreement with the essential principles espoused by the Spiritist Doctrine. We can already see this transition taking place, a prelude to the moral revival heralded by the advent of the Spiritist Doctrine.

MAXIMS AND REFLECTIONS FROM SPIRITS' WISDOM

1. The essential purpose of the Spiritist Doctrine is to improve the understanding and ethical progress of mankind.

2. The true Spiritist is not one who simply believes in spirit communications, but one who tries to learn from the ideas imparted by the spirits. A belief is barren if it doesn't lead humanity to progress or cause people to treat each other better.

3. Selfishness, pride, vanity, greed, hatred, jealousy, and slander are poisonous to the soul; we must weed these feelings out every day. Their antidotes are a spirit of love and humbleness of heart.

4. Only those of whom we can say, "Today he is a better person than he was yesterday," have benefited from their belief in the Spiritist Doctrine.

5. The importance we attribute to material goods is inversely proportional to our belief in the continuity of life. It is the doubt of a future life that leads us to indulge in worldly pleasures and seek only to satisfy our passions, often to the point that the predicament of our neighbors becomes of no concern.

6. Our tribulations on Earth are therapeutic for the soul. As far as the future life is concerned, they are like the surgery that returns an ill person to health. That is why Christ said, "Blessed are those who mourn, for they will be comforted."[47]

7. In your tribulations, look always to those below you, not those above you. Take time to show solidarity with those who suffer even more than you do.

8. Despair is natural to those who believe that everything ends with the body, but senseless to those who believe in the soul's future.

■ ■ ■

[47] *Translator's Note: Matthew 5:4*

9.   Often human beings cause their own unhappiness in this world. So often, the cause of people's problems is found in their improvidence, pride, and greed. In a nutshell, they are the result of the infringement of God's laws.

10.   A prayer is an act of worship. Praying to God means thinking of God, coming closer to God, communicating with God.

11.   Those who pray with devotion are strengthened against temptations; they receive the assistance of good spirits. It is an assistance that is never denied if it is asked with heartfelt sincerity.

12.   It's not as important to pray often, as it is to pray well. Some people believe that merit lies entirely in the length of the prayer rather than in their efforts toward self-improvement. For them, prayer is an occupation, a way of spending their time, rather than a means of examining their own imperfections, and changing themselves.

13.   When we ask for God's forgiveness, we must show a change in behavior. Good deeds are the best prayers, because actions speak louder than words.

14.   All good spirits recommend prayers. On the other hand, the afflicted ones request that others pray for them, to help lessen their suffering.

15.   Prayer can't change Providence's decree, but a suffering spirit feels less helpless, less miserable, when it sees someone interested in its fate. Prayers strengthen and inspire troubled spirits to pull themselves up through their trials, and protect them from harmful thoughts. In this sense, prayer not only lightens, but also shortens their suffering.

16.   Pray according to your beliefs and in the manner you think best, because the form is unimportant and it's the thought that counts. Sincerity and honesty of intentions are essential. A good thought is worth much more than a profusion of words that have no real depth of feeling or commitment.

17.   The stronger and better prepared are called by God to look after those who have been less fortunate. Those who selfishly ignore the needs of others will harvest the result of their neglect. Some will do it here in this life, others in a future life.

18.   Wealth is like a loan that can be called at any time. At the end of the loan, one will have to account for how it was employed.

19.   Wealth is a more dangerous test than scantness of resources, because it is a temptation to excesses. It's much harder to be moderate than to endure hardship.

20.   The greedy who amass a fortune or the rich who indulge themselves in worldly pleasures should be pitied rather than envied. They will have to account for their actions. The Spiritist Doctrine, through the vivid examples of those who lived before and who come now to tell us of their fate, confirms the truth of Christ's words, "For everyone who exalts himself will be humbled, and he who humbles himself will be exalted."[48]

21.   A duty of love is Christ's supreme message, "Love one another as brothers; love your neighbor as yourself; love your enemies; do to others what you would have them do to you; the greatest . . . is love."[49]

22.   Charity is not merely the giving of alms; it can be expressed in thoughts, words, and actions. Our thoughts are love-filled when they are tolerant of our neighbor's faults. Our words are beneficial when what we say doesn't harm others. Our actions are charitable when we help our fellow human beings to the limits of our strength.

23.   The poor person who shares his bread with one even poorer than himself is more charitable and more meritorious in God's eyes, than one who shares of his surplus without any personal sacrifice.

■ ■ ■

[48] *Translator's Note: Luke 14:11.*

■ ■ ■

[49] *Translator's Note: Luke 10:27; Mark 12:31; Luke 6:35; 1Cor. 13:13.*

24.   Those who have feelings of animosity, hatred, envy, or resentment against their fellow human beings lack in charity. They are not truthful to themselves (and others) if they call themselves Christians.

25.   All women and men are brothers and sisters regardless of race, religion, or color, because they are all called by God. Therefore, join hands, whatever the manner of your worship. Don't hurl offenses at one another, because that is a violation of the spirit of charity proclaimed by Christ.

26.   Human beings suffer inner turmoil when they are selfish, but when they are charitable, they are at peace. Happiness in this world will be assured only when brotherly kindness becomes the very foundation of human institutions. According to Christ, only love can assure future happiness, because it contains all the virtues that lead to spiritual illumination. When humankind lives the true spirit of love taught by Christ, there will no longer be selfishness, pride, hatred, envy, or slander. The inordinate pursuit of worldly goods will also disappear. This is why the highest tenet of Christian Spiritism is, **"Without love (charity), there is no salvation."**

A word to skeptics and critics! You may laugh at the notion of spirits, and mock those who believe in their manifestations. Still, the knowledge they reveal may be the armor that guarantees the permanence of life on Earth. If love were to disappear from the face of the Earth, humanity would destroy itself, and perhaps you would be among the first victims. However, we must believe that it won't be long before brotherly kindness, openly promoted by the wise spirits, will become the bond of trust among those who have it engraved in their hearts.

One spirit stated, "They made a joke of table-turning, but they will never laugh at the philosophy and life principles that arose from it." In fact, just a few years later, we already have come far from that class of phenomena. To those who say this ethical philosophy is outdated and that, "the spirits could well be a bit more spirited and bring us something new," as one critic challenged, we say, "so much the better, if it is 'old'; it merely proves that it's a timeless moral philosophy and that humanity is to blame for not practicing it."

Eternal truths are the real truths. The Spiritist Doctrine has come to remind us of them, not through an isolated revelation by a single individual, but through the voices of the spirits themselves, who proclaim, "Believe that those you thought were dead are more alive than you are, because they see what you can't see and hear what you can't hear. Know that those who have come to talk to you are your kin, your friends, and all those you loved while they lived on Earth, and thought, with their death, were lost forever. Pity those who believe that everything ends with the body's death; they are sorely mistaken. Pity those who snub the idea of living with compassion, because they will experience the same coldness they extend to others. Learn from the experiences of others. Listen to the voices of those who suffer and have come to tell you, 'We suffer because we ignored God and doubted Divine Compassion! We are suffering for our pride, our selfishness, our avarice, and all those other misguided passions we didn't repress. We suffer for the harm we caused our fellow human beings when we forgot to be compassionate.'"

A doctrine that defends such views doesn't deserve to be the subject of ridicule. Tell us what is corrupting in these principles. Also, tell us, if from the point of view of social order, those who follow it are likely to be happy or unhappy, better off or worse off.

BIOGRAPHICAL SKETCH

ALLAN KARDEC

Hippolyte Leon Denizard Rivail, who would later bear the name of Allan Kardec, was born on October 3, 1804, in Lyon, France. It was assumed that the young Rivail would follow the path of his many ancestors, who had distinguished themselves as lawyers and magistrates. However, he was attracted from his youth to the sciences and philosophy.

Denizard Rivail completed his early studies at Yverdun, Switzerland, where he became the disciple and collaborator of the celebrated Professor Pestalozzi. He then applied himself whole-heartedly to the propagation of the education system championed by Pestalozzi, which came to have a great influence on the French and German school systems. When Pestalozzi received requests from governments to establish institutes similar to that of Yverdun, he often conferred the direction of these new schools upon Rivail. The disciple-turned-teacher had acquired all the requisite qualifications for such a task: he had a Bachelor of Arts degree in letters and science, and a doctorate in medicine. Furthermore, a remarkable linguist, he spoke German, English, Italian, and Spanish fluently and could easily express himself in Dutch.

His interest in letters and pedagogy often brought Rivail to Paris, where he met Amelia Boudet, a professor nine years his senior. They were married on February 6, 1832.

Rivail founded a Technical Institute in Paris similar to the one in Yverdun. His partner, his mother's brother, had a passion for gambling which ultimately led to the liquidation of the Institute. Rivail and his wife invested their share of the liquidation, 45,000 francs, into the business of an intimate friend, a merchant who did poorly and who, at his death, left nothing to his creditors.

Far from discouraged by his repeated misfortune, Rivail found work managing the accounting for three companies, which brought him about 7,000 francs a year. In the evening, after his day's work was done, he wrote books about grammar, arithmetic, and higher pedagogical studies, and he translated English and German works into French. From 1835 to 1840, he also designed and taught courses in chemistry, physics, astronomy, physiology, and comparative anatomy.

Rivail was a member of various scholarly societies, most notably the Royal Academy of Arras, and his presentation of his noteworthy article, "Which System of Study Is Most Harmonious with the Needs of the Time?" won a competition in 1831. His numerous works also include *A Plan for the Improvement of Public Instruction*, presented in 1828; *Practical and Theoretical Course of Arithmetic*, published in 1824 for mothers and teachers; *Classical French Grammar*, published in 1831; a manual of examinations taken to obtain professional diplomas, and the solutions to questions and problems in arithmetic and geometry; *Grammatical Catechism of the French Language*, published in 1848; and *Normal Dictations of Examinations in the Municipality* and the Sorbonne and *Special Dictations About Orthographic Difficulties*, both published in 1849.

Rivail received income from the sale of these diverse works to French universities, and the very rapid exposure that resulted prepared him for the demanding enterprise he would eventually undertake. His name was known and respected and his works justly appreciated long before he was immortalized as Allan Kardec.

Had he simply continued in his academic career, Rivail would've been able to live an honored, happy, and tranquil life. His fortune was reconstructed through his persevering work and the brilliant success that crowned his efforts, but his mission called him to a more burdensome occupation. His dispositions and aspirations might have inclined him toward mysticism, but his education, candid judgment, and methodical observation provided a balance and prevented him from resorting to enthusiastic extremes or unjustified skepticism.

Rivail first heard of rapping tables in 1854. He was introduced to the phenomenon by Mr. Fortier, a hypnotist with whom Rivail was acquainted through his studies of human magnetism.[50] One day, Fortier said to him, "Here is a thing that is quite extraordinary. Not only is a table made to tilt, but it can also be made to speak. Ask it a question, and it replies."

"That," Rivail replied, "is not magnetism, but another matter. I will believe it when I see it, and when it has been proved to me that a table has a brain to think and nerves to feel and that it can become an experimental subject. Until then, allow me to see nothing in this but a fable." Such was Rivail's position. He never denied a thing on preconceived opinions, but he always asked for proof, wanting to observe and analyze before taking a position.

Here is how Allan Kardec reveals his doubts and hesitations and his first initiation to the rapping tables:

I found myself, then, confronted with an unexplained fact that was, in appearance, contrary to the laws of nature and that my reason rejected. I had not yet seen or investigated anything; the experiments done in the presence of honorable and trustworthy people had at least confirmed for me the possibility of the purely material effect, but the idea of a talking table still did not enter my mind.

The following year, in the beginning of 1855, I met Mr. Carlotti, with whom I maintained a friendship for twenty-five years. For more than an hour, he discoursed about those phenomena with all the enthusiasm he reserved for new ideas. He was of Corsican origin and, by

■ ■ ■

[50] *Translator's Note: Allan Kardec was a serious investigator of a phenomenon that intrigued some of the great scientists of his time—the effect of the mind on physical healing. The field evolved into what is known today as hypnosis. The history of modern hypnosis begins in the Eighteenth Century with the arrival of Franz Anton Mesmer (1734–1815). Portuguese monk, Abbe Faria (1756-1819), learned to produce a somnambulist state simply by gazing steadily at the patient and then shouting "Sleep!" Dr. James Braid (1795–1869) coined the word 'hypnotism' after the Greek god of sleep, Hypnos, to describe the art and science of inducing hypnosis. Support for the teaching of the therapeutic use of hypnosis in medicine finally came in 1955 from the British Medical Association, and was closely followed in 1958 by the American Medical Association. It has received bad press since, mainly due to the unscrupulous practices of some stage hypnotists, but its professional use in treating both physical and mental disorders continues to thrive.*

nature, ardent and energetic; I had always distinguished in him the qualities that characterize a great and beautiful soul, but his enthusiasm made me skeptical. He was the first to speak to me about the intervention of the spirits, and he told me many surprising things that, far from convincing me, increased my doubts. "One day you will join us," he told me. "I do not deny it," I replied. "We will see about that later."

Some time afterward, in May 1855, I was in the home of Mrs. Roger, with Fortier, a hypnotist. There, I met Mr. Patier and Mrs. Plainemaison, who spoke to me about those phenomena in the same vein as Carlotti. Patier was a public servant of advanced age, a well-educated man of serious character, analytical and calm. His language, deliberate and devoid of any enthusiasm, made a strong impression on me and, when he invited me to attend the experiments that took place in Mrs. Plainemaison's home at Grange Batelier Street, n. 18, I anxiously accepted. The meeting was set for Tuesday at 8 o'clock in the evening.

It was there that I witnessed for the first time the phenomenon of rapping tables, which jumped and moved under conditions that precluded doubt.

It was also there that I saw some very imperfect attempts at mediumistic writing on a slate with the help of a basket. My ideas were far from being modified, but I saw in that phenomenon an effect that must have had a cause. I glimpsed, beneath the apparent frivolities and entertainment associated with these phenomena, something serious, perhaps the revelation of a new law, which I promised myself I would explore.

The occasion to do so was soon offered to me. At one of Mrs. Plainemaison's soirees, I became acquainted with the Baudin family, who lived then at Rochechouart Street. Mr. Baudin invited me to attend the weekly meeting held at his home, and I accepted. I have been returning regularly ever since.

These meetings provided me with my first opportunity for serious studies of the subject that later led to the Spiritist Doctrine—study filled less with revelation and more with systematic observation. As to any new subject, I applied rigorous method to the investigation: avoiding preconceived notions, I observed attentively, compared observations, and deduced the consequences. I tried to identify the causes of the phenomena by linking the facts logically, and I did not accept an explanation as valid unless it could resolve all the difficulties of the question. This was the way I had always, from the age of fif-

teen or sixteen, proceeded in my investigations. *I understood from the beginning the gravity of the exploration I was undertaking. I foresaw in those phenomena, the key to the solution of problems so obscure and so disputed, both in the past and in the future, which I had searched for all my life; the phenomena posed a complete revolution in ideas and beliefs. It was necessary, therefore, to act not lightly, but rather with circumspection, to be positive rather than idealistic, so as not to be carried away by illusions.*

One of my first observations was that the spirits, being only the souls of men and women, did not have either absolute wisdom or absolute knowledge; their knowledge was limited to the level of their advancement and their remarks had only the value of a personal opinion. Recognizing this fact from the beginning saved me from the serious error of believing in the spirits' infallibility, and prevented me from formulating premature theories based upon the opinion of only one or a few spirits.

The mere fact of communication with the spirits, no matter what they said, proved the existence of an invisible world. This, in itself, was a fantastic discovery, opening an immense field for exploration and providing a key to understanding a multitude of unexplained phenomena. No less important, it furnished the means to understand the state of that world and its customs, if we may thus call them. I observed early on that each spirit, with its own personal position and knowledge, unveiled to me an aspect of that world, just as one comes to know about a country by interrogating inhabitants of all classes and circumstances, each able to impart something and none able, individually, to impart everything. Any observer is obliged to form a picture of the whole by examining the material collected from different sources, which he must compile, coordinate, and compare. I, then, dealt with the spirits as I would have dealt with human subjects; from the lowest to the most elevated, they were, for me, simply a means of gathering information, not infallible experts.

To these statements, gathered from the *Posthumous Works,*[51] it is important to add that, at the beginning, Rivail was far from

■■■

[51] *Translator's Note: The book, Posthumous Works, published a few years after his death, offers a collection of Allan Kardec's finest reflective writings about the organization and future of the Spiritist movement. In addition, it presents an insightful study about the historical Jesus, based on how Jesus saw and referred to himself in the Gospels.*

being an enthusiast of those experiences and was absorbed by other occupations. He might even have abandoned his investigation had it not been for the insistent solicitations of Carlotti, Rene Taillander, a member of the French Academy of Sciences, Tiedeman-Manthese, Mr. Sardou and his son, and Mr. Didier, a publisher. They had studied the phenomena for five years and compiled fifty notebooks of diverse communications, which they had not been able to put in order. Aware of Rivail's great aptitude for synthesis, these gentlemen sent the notebooks to him, requesting him to acquaint himself with them and arrange them in some order. This arduous job demanded much time because of the omissions and obscurities in those communications, and Rivail, the wise encyclopedist, refused this boring and absorbing task, preferring to work on other pursuits.

One night, his spirit guide, who identified itself as "Z.," gave him a completely personal communication through a medium. Rivail was told, among other things, that Z. had known him in a previous existence during the time of the Druids;[52] they had lived together in Gaul. At that time, Rivail was named Allan Kardec. Since the friendship Z. had vowed to Kardec had only increased, Z. promised to support him in the very important task he was called to do, and which, Z. assured him, he would easily carry to completion.

Rivail then threw himself into the work. He took the notebooks and annotated them carefully. He deleted repetitions and put each dictation in its respective sequence, each exposition ordered by session; he also noted the omissions to be filled out, the obscurities to be clarified, and prepared the questions necessary to fill the gaps. Rivail, himself, said,

Until then, the sessions at Baudin's home had no deliberate purpose whatsoever. I proposed, therefore, to resolve the problems in philosophy, psychology, and the nature of the invisible world that interested me. I arrived at each session with a series of questions prepared

■ ■ ■

[52] *Translator's Note: The Druids were the wise men of the Celtic people. They were thought to be philosophers, priests, educators, doctors, seers, and astronomers. They enjoyed a position of high status in the society. The Celtic people thrived in pre-Christian times in the British Isles.*

and methodically proposed; they were answered with precision, depth, and in a logical manner. From that moment, the meetings began to have a very different character, and some attendees were serious people who took lively interest in the work. If I happened to be absent from a session, the excitement was dampened; futile questions had lost their charm for the majority of attendees. At the beginning, I had in mind only my own task. Later, when I saw that everything formed a whole and took on the proportions of a system, I decided to publish the proceedings of the meetings for everyone's edification.

I was not satisfied with the verification processes, however; I wanted outside confirmation. Circumstances put me into contact with other mediums, and I took advantage of every occasion to propose some of the questions that seemed to me most open to further explanation. In this way, more than ten mediums cooperated in this work. By comparing and merging all the replies I thus received, which were coordinated, classified, and often revised in the silence of meditation, I formed the first edition of The Spirits' Book, *which appeared on April 18, 1857.*

The book was so successful that the first edition sold out immediately. Rivail, using the name Allan Kardec, revised, corrected, and considerably augmented the work in 1858.

Spurred on by the success of *The Spirits' Book* and the other documents he had in his possession, Allan Kardec decided to create a monthly journal called *Revue Spirite*. He requested financial backing from Tiedeman-Mantese, who was not willing to take part in such a business. Kardec then asked his guides, on November 15, 1857, through Miss E. Dufaux, what he should do. He was informed that he should put his idea into action and not worry about the rest.

"Without saying anything to anybody," said Kardec, "I hurried to edit the first issue. It appeared on the first of January 1858. I had no assistant, nor a financial partner. I did it, then, entirely at my own cost and risk, and I had no cause to regret my action; the success surpassed my expectations. The subsequent issues followed each other without interruption, and, as the spirit had foreseen, the review became a powerful auxiliary to my efforts. I realized later that the lack of a financial partner was actually a blessing—I was freer than I would have been if an interested outsider had attempted to impose his ideas and will upon me, hindering my progress. Alone, I did not have to account to anybody, no matter how burdensome my task may have been."

And the burden of Kardec's task did increase, both in terms of the amount of labor and responsibility, and in regard to the constant struggles against obstacles, dishonest associates, and risks of every kind. As difficult leadership issues emerged, the energetic man rose to the challenge; nothing ever surprised him. During the eleven years he published the *Revue Spirite*, he confronted and dispensed with all the storms, rivalries, and jealousies he encountered. The following communication, delivered through a medium, Aline C., on June 12, 1856, and the reflections noted below it by Allan Kardec, show us the situation he faced at that time, but it also heightens the great worth of Allan Kardec and his ability to triumph.

Allan Kardec: What are the causes that could make me fail? Would it be the insufficiency of my aptitudes?

Spirit of truth:[53] No. But the path of reformers is full of rocks and dangers, and yours is rough. I forewarn you because you are trying to agitate and transform the way the world thinks. Don't think that it is sufficient to publish one book, two books, ten books, and to remain tranquilly at home; no, it's necessary for you to show yourself in the conflict. Terrible hates will be incited against you; implacable enemies will plot your downfall. You will be exposed to calumny and treachery, even from those who seem most dedicated to you. Your best works will be condemned and banned. You will succumb more than once to fatigue. You will have to sustain an almost con-

■ ■ ■

[53] *Translator's Note: Spirit of truth – concept explained in the glossary.*

stant struggle, sacrificing your rest, your tranquillity, your health, and even your life, because you will not live a long life. Well then. More than one person recoils when, instead of a flower-strewn path, he finds only thorns, sharp rocks, and serpents beneath his feet. For missions such as yours, intelligence is not enough. To please God, it is necessary above all to have humility, modesty, and selflessness. To struggle against human beings, courage is also necessary. Prudence and tact are called for, so as to conduct things according to the purpose and not to compromise success by inopportune means or words. Finally, devotion, self-denial, and readiness for all sacrifices are required. You see that the success of your mission is subordinated to conditions that depend upon you.

REFLECTIONS BY ALLAN KARDEC

I am writing this note on January 1, 1867, ten and a half years after the communication above was given to me, and I verify that all its predictions were realized; I experienced all the difficulties that were announced in it. I have been the target of the hate of implacable enemies, of insult, of calumny, of envy, and of jealousy. Infamous libels have been published against me, and my best work and teachings have been attacked. I have been betrayed by those whom I trusted, and paid with ingratitude by those to whom I have given my best. The Societe Spirite de Paris (Spiritist Society of Paris) has been a continuous focus of intrigues, devised by those who declared loyalty and friendship to me, but who slandered me in my absence. They said that I paid those who favored my work with money I received from Spiritism. I have known no peace, and more than once I succumbed; under the excess of work, my health has deteriorated and my life has been compromised.

However, thanks to the protection and assistance of good spirits, who have ceaselessly given me manifest proof of their solicitude, I am happy to recognize that I have not experienced a

single moment of weakness nor discouragement. I have perse-
vered in my task with the same ardor, without worrying myself
about the hatred to which I was the target. Everything predicted
in the communication of the Spirit of truth has come to pass.

Hippolyte Leon Denizard Rivail, also known as Allan
Kardec, died in Paris from an aneurysm on March 31, 1869, at
the age of 65. His remains rest in the cemetery of Pere
Lachaise in Paris, beneath an impressive Druid-style stone
structure erected by his followers. His grave is a point of reference in the foremost cemetery of Paris. His is the only site
adorned with fresh flowers year round, a tribute to a man
whose work reestablished the primacy of the spirit in the
human journey.

GLOSSARY

Action and Reaction—see Cause and Effect.

Afterlife — the life after the physical life; the state to which the spirit returns after existence in the physical realm.

Angel — a being that has attained the state of pure spirit. Angels have passed up through all the degrees on the scale of progress and freed themselves from all the impurities of material worlds.

Animism — a situation in which the medium's subconscious mind, rather than another spiritual individuality, is the source of a mediumistic message. The term is also used to identify religious practices based in the belief that all living things have a soul. However, only the former notion is recognized in the Spiritist literature.

Apparition — the phenomenon through which a spirit becomes visible to the naked eye.

Astral Body — see Perispirit.

Attachment (Spirit) — a temporary situation in which spirits of limited awareness seek connection and enjoy living in close relationship with an incarnate person.

Aura — a field of energy that surrounds human beings. The aura is a form of radiation emitted by the spirit. It should not be confused with the bio-energy that radiates from the human and animal body.

Automatic Writing (Psychography) — the process of receiving written communications without the control of the conscious self. Writing of the truly automatic kind, when the arm and hand are under spirit control, is rare. More often, the writing is the product of mind-to-mind communication between the medium and the communicating spirit. By its very nature, the process may be more or less affected by the medium's mind.

Bio-energy — the vital life force that sustains physical life (see also Vitalism).

Catalepsy — a condition in which consciousness and feeling are suddenly, temporarily lost, and muscles become rigid; it may occur in epilepsy and schizophrenia.

Cause and Effect (Action and Reaction) — a law of nature according to which every effect must have a generating cause. In the moral realm, every conscious human action produces an effect. Logically, good actions are likely to generate good reactions, and vice-versa. In the ultimate sense, however, the effect is more than just an equivalent outcome. For instance, a person who seriously harms another doesn't need, necessarily, to experience the same form of harm, because the person may neutralize the negative effect by doing good to others. This interpretation of the principle of cause and effect is more attuned with Jesus' instruction "For she loved much, her sins are forgiven" (Luke 7:47), and the concept of Divine Justice.

Christian Spiritist — the person who sympathizes with or embraces the spirit philosophy, and is committed to the work of personal transformation following the ideal defined by Jesus Christ.

Christianity — Christian beliefs or practices; Christian qualities or character. In the Spiritist tradition, Christianity defines a mental attitude and a relationship with life in all its expressions, rather than a religion in the conventional sense of the word.

Clairaudience — a paranormal perception in which the person hears spirit voices within the mind and perceives events taking place in the spirit realm.

Clairvoyance — a paranormal kind of perception in which the human mind perceives images, more or less well defined, of events, scenes, or objects in the spirit realm.

Cord (Spiritual) — see Silver Cord.

Cosmic Principle — the subtle, fundamental, unifying substance that gives rise to phenomena such as heat, magnetism, and electricity, and to matter itself.

Cult — a religion or religious sect regarded as unorthodox, with its followers often living in an unconventional manner under the guidance of an authoritarian, charismatic leader.

Death — the exhaustion of the bodily organs and with that, the complete liberation of the spirit from the physical body.

Demons — spirits of scanty moral progress who nurture hatred and harbor base sentiments and inclinations.

Destiny — a predetermined course of events in human life. The Spiritist Doctrine does not endorse the view that the circumstances of a person's life were scripted beforehand. They are usually the result of a person's own actions, or choices made before incarnation. Human beings are the creators of their own destiny.

Determinism — the notion that every event, including human choices and decisions, have sufficient causes. The Spiritist philosophy does not support this view in all that regards the moral and spiritual aspects of human life.

Devil — same as demon.

Divine Justice — the system of laws and norms that flow from God. They are eternal and unchanging. The Divine Justice assures that every person receives according to his or her merit. It is not a strict system of punishments and rewards. God always considers the causes of our actions and does not punish any one. Love is the fundamental essence of the Divine Justice.

Dreams — dreams are often the recollection of what the spirit experiences, or of what happens during sleep of the body. The spirit is never inactive during the bodily rest. The dreams referred to in the original works of the Spiritist Doctrine are known, in modern dream literature, as psychic dreams.

Ecstatic trance — a state of profound inner concentration in which the person shows little awareness of the immediate environment. In this state, the person may have visions and manifest special mediumistic powers. It is distinguished by an intense feeling of joy.

Ectoplasm (From the Greek: ektos, external, and plasma, substance) — visible substance that exhales from the body of certain mediums in the production of materializations.

Eternal punishment — the belief in certain religions that all wrongdoers are banished by God to a place of perpetual suffering. Such a notion is strongly rejected by the Spiritist Doctrine. See also Hell and Hellfire.

Euthanasia — the act of interrupting human life in a painless manner to, supposedly, relieve the pain and suffering of a terminal illness. From a continuous life perspective, euthanasia generates a complex stream of consequences that may bring more suffering than the person still had to endure.

Evil Spirits — same as demons.

Evolution (Spiritual) — the process of development of the spirit. Spirits were created simple and in a state of unawareness. They develop and grow through experiences in this and various other spheres of life. The spirit's evolution is a continuous and progressive movement. Evolution is a forward movement, it never regresses. Every spirit has to tread the path of evolution; none is left behind or condemned to unawareness.

Exorcism — ritual ceremonies or formulas used by certain religions to remove a harmful or disturbing spirit from a place or a person's life.

Expiation — the means and circumstances by which a person atones, or provides reparation, for wrongs done to self or others. Used in the Spiritist literature to refer to experiences in which there is a great deal of suffering or difficulty, unconnected to a person's past actions or choices during earthly life.

Extra Sensorial Perception — see Paranormality.

Family (Spiritual) — any group of spirit beings that share mutual affection, and have affinity of ideas and values. They may choose to be born in the same family of kin. Their connections have roots in past life experiences. This affinity may draw these spirits together in the physical life. Their ties strengthen with their progress.

Fatalism — same as determinism.

Fate — same as destiny.

Free spirits — the temporary state of spirits between incarnations.

Free will — the notion that human action expresses personal choice, rather than the intervention of Divine forces. Free will is a fundamental right of the human consciousness. Without free will, human life would be either a series of predetermined movements or a sequence of random events. As a spirit progresses, the exercise, so to speak, of its free will expands, i.e., the spirit takes responsibility for a wider range of choices.

Gender (in spirits) — spirits have no gender in the strict sense of the word, however, they may retain for large periods of time the psychological characteristics of a man or woman. The identification with a particular gender dies away in proportion to the spirit's purification.

Ghost — in the popular culture, a word used in reference to the soul of a dead person that wanders among or haunts living persons. Such occurrences are indeed the sighting of the spiritual body, or perispirit, of those persons who, after their physical death, are temporarily unable to adjust themselves to the spirit realm.

Gift (spiritual) — a special sensorial ability, usually identified as paranormal, that allows a person to interact with subtler dimensions of life, i.e., spirit reality.

God — the Supreme Intelligence of the Universe, the First Cause of all things.

Golden Rule — "Do to others as you would have them do to you" (Luke 6:31).

Guardian Angel — same as guide.

Guide (Spiritual) — a spirit who has achieved a high stage, relatively speaking, of ethical and intellectual development. They may be identified as teachers, guides, or counselors. They take an interest in the growth of an individual or group. Other schools of thought call them angels, and spiritual masters.

Healing (Spiritual) — treatment of physical or spiritual illnesses by means of bio-energy transfer and prayer. Through cleansing or replenishing the energies of the spiritual body, the physical body is able to restore itself to health. The healer works in close association with spiritual beings. The therapy is based on the power of prayer, faith, and love.

Healing Energy — the energy that enables spiritual healing to take place. It is the energy produced through prayer and faith during the spiritual healing therapy. See also Healing.

Hell — in traditional Christian theology, the place in which evil doers are condemned to live for all eternity. The Spiritist philosophy rejects the notion of hell as a place of perpetual punishment because all God's creatures are destined to progress and attain happiness. In Spiritist literature, the word hell is employed only as metaphor to describe a place where distraught, rebellious, and angry souls gather temporarily.

Hellfire — the notion of hellfire, considered as a punishment for wrongdoers, dates back to ancient times, tracing its origins to the primitive belief that hell was physically located deep under the Earth. See hell above.

Hypnotic Power — the power held by certain individuals, as well as spirit beings, to induce another into a hypnotic state.

Hypnotism — the science of dealing with the induction of hypnosis, an artificially induced state resembling sleep in which the subject is highly susceptible to suggestion.

Incarnate Spirit — a spirit that is temporarily wearing the garment of a physical body; the soul of a living person.

Induced Trance — usually a self-induced trance in preparation for mediumistic, psychic practice.

Innate Ideas — ideas or knowledge that one is seemingly born with. The spiritist philosophy places their origin in the spirit's previous lives.

Inner Transformation — the renovation of moral values, views, and behavior that constitutes the essential purpose of incarnate life. It is the striving to acquire the perfections inspired by becoming conscious of God. The enlightened spirits who dictated the Spiritist Doctrine considered inner transformation as the fundamental task of the spirit in the course of time, and have presented Jesus as our Divine point of reference.

Inner Voice — the voice of conscience in its purest expression. St. Francis of Assisi used this expression to identify the Christ voice that guided him in critical decisions.

Intelligent Principle — one of the essential principles of the universe; the core constituent of the spirit.

Intuition — the ability to understand a situation or draw conclusions about complex events without the use of sensory process. Also, a form of presentiment about future events. For some spiritually sensitive persons, the ability to sense the ideations of enlightened spirits who take interest in a particular area of human development.

Invocation — the act of invoking a spirit being, Jesus, or God, for aid, protection, inspiration, or guidance.

Jesus — in the words of the enlightened spirits who laid the basis of Christian Spiritism as a philosophy of life, "the most perfect example that God has offered to us as a guide and model."

Karma — Hindu and Buddhist ethical principle of "as one sows, so shall one reap" in this or in a future reincarnation. According to the law of karma, every conscious human action—in thought, word, or deed—leads to consequences, good or bad, depending on the quality of the action. Karma implies strict causality. A positive act will lead to a positive result. Accordingly, the result will directly correspond to the nature of the cause. In the Christian Spiritist application, the notion of direct causality between the action and the result of the action is amended with Jesus' precept "For she loved much, her sins are forgiven" (Luke 7:47). See Cause and Effect.

Kirlian — a photographic method that captures bio-fields of persons or objects through a high-voltage discharge process. The process of Kirlian photography is named after Seymon Kirlian, a Russian inventor. The interpretation of the coronas that surround the animate objects photographed is open to controversy. Some researchers argue that they are a paranormal phenomenon, the aura. Others counter that they show nothing more than electricity being discharged, which can be produced under certain conditions. Although we are far from a conclusive interpretation, there is growing evidence that energy flows in the body are influenced by mental states, medical conditions, healing treatment, prayer, etc.

Last Judgment — according to the traditional dogma, "the final trial of all mankind." This notion is not supported in the Christian Spiritist philosophy because the Doctrine views the process of life and evolution as continuous and infinite.

Laying On of Hands — a form of spiritual healing in which the healer, in a state of profound meditation or prayer, places hands over the patient's head without physical touch. In this state, the healer gives off the bio-energy that replenishes or helps rebalance the patient's energy field. This is the purest form of spiritual healing—it was practiced by Jesus.

Levitation — the raising of a person or object through psychic or paranormal methods.

Magnetic Healing — similar to Spiritual Healing but reliant only on the energy and mental power of the healer (as opposed to healing with the assistance of spiritual guides, and prayer).

Magnetism — the human power to induce a hypnotic state. This capability was believed to be at the base of mesmeric phenomena, a precursor of modern hypnotism. Nineteenth Century scientific opinions about the cause of the phenomenon ranged from "the existence of an animal emanation or never-force" (J.P.F. Deluze) to "mental suggestion" (Abbe Aria). The modern notion of energy fields may bring scientific acceptance to the concept of sharing and transfer of energy between living beings. See also Mesmerism.

Materialism — the philosophical principle that matter is the only reality and all phenomena, including thought and feeling, can be explained in terms of matter and physical processes. Alternatively used to signify the attitude that possessions are the greatest good and highest value of life, and that spiritual values are not relevant.

Materialization — one of the several types of mediumistic phenomena produced by conscious or unconscious mediums who possess such a gift. During materialization, a spirit takes a visible form to make itself materially visible.

Medium (from the Latin: medium, intermediate) — a person endowed with a superior sensitivity who serves as an intermediary for communication between the physical and spirit world.

Mediumship — the faculty of mediums. There are many types of mediumship. The more common are: trance, automatic writing, and clairvoyance.

Mentor — same as guide.

Mesmerism — a healing method developed by F. A. Mesmer (1733–1815) involving the inducement of hypnotic trances and the transfer of physical energy, originally named animal magnetism, from the therapist to the patient. People in trance often showed paranormal abilities.

Metempsychosis — the ancient doctrine, still accepted today by certain branches of Hinduism and Buddhism, by which a soul (spirit) may enter another human body or that of an animal, according to its deeds in a previous life. The word derives from the Greek *meta* (over) and *empsychoum* (to put a soul into).

Miracle — a physical event that appears inexplicable by the known laws of nature and is considered of divine or supernatural cause. Christian Spiritism proposes that the so-called miracles, even the more amazing healing and paranormal phenomena, appear so as the result of our still limited understanding of the laws of nature.

Mission (Spiritual) — the kind of assignment trusted to more advanced spirits, as opposed to the trials and expiations experienced by the majority of the souls on Earth. Missions are attributions that impact a large circle of people, rather than just the individual or the individual's immediate family.

Moral Conscience — a well-developed ability to understand right from wrong coupled with a resilient willingness to act accordingly. To act in such a manner requires cultivation of emotions and integration of spiritual values in the management of physical needs and desires.

Obsession — in Spiritist studies, the temporary influence exercised by an ill-meaning spirit over a person. The causes range from a person's own behavior all the way to mutual hatred between the besetting spirit and its victim, and may have origin in this, as well as in a previous lifetime. It is a condition that requires spiritual treatment, behavior change, and inner transformation. In severe cases, it may cause physical and mental ailments.

Occult — related to magic, astrology, and other disciplines that rely on secret, mysterious, or supernatural forces.

Oracle — in Greek mythology, the response typically given through a priestess (who served as medium) to a question put to the gods. Such responses were often enigmatic and interpreted by the temple authorities according to the circumstances. The term oracle was also used to refer to the priestess herself, as well as to the place of worship and consultation of a deity and the related phenomena.

Original Sin — in traditional Christian theology, the sin committed by Adam, the first man. As a consequence of this first sin, we are all born with a tendency to be evil. This notion is not endorsed by the Spiritist Doctrine, which postulates that all spirits are created equal, with the same propensity for good and wrong.

Out-of-Body Experience (OBE) — the temporary freedom obtained by an incarnate spirit during deep trance or sleep to travel outside the human body. The spirit may visit places or friends on Earth, travel to places in the spirit realm, or take part in benevolent endeavors under the guidance of a spiritual mentor.

Paradise — in traditional Christian theology, the abode of the righteous in the afterlife. In the Spiritist Doctrine, the notion of paradise or heaven is not circumscribed to a specific location; it is a metaphor to describe the state of mind of enlightened spirits, wherever they may be, because they are free from all moral anguish and anxieties that characterize less enlightened individuals.

Paranormality — deals with events beyond the range of normal sensorial experience or scientific explanation; for instance, a medium's intuition of a future event.

Perispirit (from the Greek, perí means surrounding) — it is the subtle body of the spirit. It serves as interface between the spirit and the physical body. Also known as spiritual body, astral body, or double.

Poltergeist — a paranormal phenomenon involving the movement of objects, rapping, and sounds produced by spiritual entities. Usually the presence of a person with the proper type of sensitivity is necessary for the phenomena to occur.

Polytheism — the belief in the existence of more than one god.

Possession (Spiritual) — an aggravated spiritual obsession (see Obsession) in which the ill-meaning spirit is able to have a controlling influence over a person's actions. Spiritual possession tends to have a longer course. Deep-seated hatred or vengeance are usually the motivating forces behind these relationships. Cure requires spiritual assistance and specialized medical treatment.

Premonition — an intuitive anticipation of a future event.

Psychometry — a psychic gift with which the medium is able to sense the history of an object by holding it, or the past of a person by simply touching or shaking hands with that person.

Pure Spirits — beings that have reached the higher states of ethical and intellectual perfection.

Purgatory — according to the theology of some traditional Christian denominations, the place of temporary punishment reserved for the penitent souls that had their sins forgiven on Earth. The Spiritist Doctrine does not subscribe to this view.

Regression (Past Lives) — psychological therapy by which persons under hypnotic trance access memories of events that have supposedly taken place in past lives. It has been successfully used in the treatment of phobias and a variety of traumatic experiences. Although not without controversy, this therapy is receiving increasing attention from the medical community.

Reincarnation — the notion that a spirit (soul) can be reborn in a new body, as part of the continuous progress toward higher levels of spiritual existence. The purpose of reincarnation is to offer the spirit opportunities to grow in awareness, love, and intellectual ability. In addition, reincarnation provides the time and circumstances for the spirit to make reparation for wrongs committed in prior existences.

Remote View — a type of psychic technique in which the medium, or subject, is able to acquire information about a person, place, or event which is distant in time or space.

Resurrection — in traditional Christian theology, the belief that, at a point in time, there will be a final judgment and God will then raise into heaven all the saved who have been dead. When this occurs, their physical bodies will rise from being dead and will be reunited with their souls. The Spiritist Doctrine does not subscribe to this view.

Revelation — the act of revealing Divine truth, or that which is revealed by God to man. Revelation is the supernatural communication of truth to the mind of a teacher or writer, who, in traditional Biblical lexicon, is called a prophet. The Spiritist Doctrine was given to humanity by ennobled intelligences who fulfilled a design of God. According to this notion, the Spiritist Doctrine is a revelation of our true spiritual nature, purpose, and destiny as eternal spirits. However, the Spiritist philosophy endorses the notion that revelation is a continuous process, and that the progress of humanity is accomplished by the incarnation of exceptional individuals with responsibilities in every major field of human endeavor, to reveal or expand continuously the frontiers of our knowledge (see *The Spirits' Book* question 622). The Doctrine in no way claims to have access to the absolute truth. This enlightened stance is cemented in the motto: "the only unshakeable faith is that which can withstand reason, face to face, in every stage of humankind's development." Besides, Allan Kardec made it a cornerstone of Spiritist thought that the Doctrine is dynamic and that its evolution should occur always in agreement with the development of scientific knowledge.

Ritual — the repeated performance of ceremonial acts prescribed by tradition or religion. Religious rituals are dependent upon some common belief system. Rituals are part of the fabric of every human society.

Second Sight — same as clairvoyance. It gives the medium the ability to see spirits and perceive events and circumstances of the spirit world. It is a complex and difficult gift in which the medium is responsible for interpreting and communicating what is seen. Because of this element of intellectual interpretation, which opens the doors to personal biases and beliefs, the issue of reliability is always a concern.

Seer — a person endowed with the gift of clairvoyance or second sight.

Sibyl — one of a number of women regarded as oracles or prophets by the ancient Greeks and Romans. See also oracle.

Silver Cord — the metaphorical link between the spiritual and the physical body. When the cord is broken, the physical body dies, and the spirit is free to continue life in the spirit world.

Sin — in religious theology, willful and deliberate transgression of Divine Law, the violation of some religious or moral principle.

Sin (Original) — see Original Sin.

Sorcery — use of supernatural (paranormal) powers over others, typically with the assistance of unenlightened spirits; divination by the assistance, or pretended assistance, of ill-meaning spirits; the power of commanding ill-meaning spirits; black magic; witchcraft.

Soul — an incarnate spirit (question 134 in this book). Before uniting to the body, the soul is one of the many distinct beings inhabiting the invisible world.

Spirit of truth (The) — in the Christian Spiritist perspective, a collective of enlightened spirits who represent the purest aspect of Christian thought and ideal. The ideas proposed in messages signed by "the Spirit of truth," in this book and other works, are Divine in a logical sense, if one considers that these ideas were produced by beings who lived in oneness with Jesus, and are inspired purely by their love of God. In the Spiritist Doctrine, "the Spirit of truth" reaffirms the morality of the Gospel as the highest creation of human conscience, and encourages the quest for knowledge through science and reason.

Spirit World — the essential world that preexists and survives everything else. Spirits are everywhere in the universe. The spirit world has beauty, life, and harmony beyond anything that incarnate beings can conceive.

Spiritist (or Christian Spiritist) — a follower of the Spiritist Doctrine.

Spiritist Doctrine or Christian Spiritism — the philosophy that deals with the nature, the origin, and the destiny of spirits, as well as their relationship with the corporeal world.

Spirits — the intelligent beings of creation. They populate the entire universe and can be found beyond the boundaries of the material world.

Spiritual Body — see perispirit.

Spiritual Family — see family.

Spiritual purity — in the Spiritist Doctrine, the state of pure spirits, who no longer have the need to reincarnate, having already experienced and learned through many lives in the physical realm.

Spiritualism — in philosophy, the notion that human beings are more than just matter. As a philosophy, Spiritualism denies that the contents of the universe are limited to matter and the properties and operations of matter. It maintains that the real being (spirit) is radically distinct in nature from matter. Plato is practically considered as the father of spiritualism, as he articulated the distinction between the irrational, or sensuous, and the rational functions of the soul. For him, the rational soul was related to the body merely as the pilot to the ship or the rider to his horse. In this sense, all religions that accept the existence in the human being of a principle independent from matter, are spiritualist.

Spiritualism, in daily American and British usage, however, is commonly defined as a belief that the dead communicate with the living through mediums. In this case, the usage is more closely associated with the religion of Modern Spiritualism. While there are many parallels between Modern Spiritualism and the Spiritist Doctrine, the differences are very significant, and they should not be confused, or used as equivalents.

Spontaneous Trance — the individual is temporarily without control of his will or awareness; commonly observed in the religious ecstasy that accompanies the phenomenon of speaking in tongues.

Suicide — the deliberate taking of one's own life. Suicide is an act that carries profound and long-lasting consequences for the spirit, as it is a transgression of the laws of nature.

Superstition — a belief, practice, or rite irrationally maintained by ignorance of the laws of nature or by faith in magic or chance.

Table Turning — the phenomenon where tables and other objects move without human contact. Table turning was very popular in the mid-1850s. The phenomenon was characterized by a table moving in irregular ways, in various directions, rising, and remaining suspended in the air. The invisible agents that produced the table movements later identified themselves as spirits. In the context of Modern Spiritualism and the Spiritist Doctrine, the tables provided the first and crudest form of communication with the spirit world. The methods of communication have since changed. Tables are no longer employed as means of communication, as other more reliable and accurate methods have become available; for instance, automatic writing and clairvoyance.

Telepathy — communication between minds without the use of ordinary sensory channels.

Theism — belief in the existence of God or gods.

Tiptology — a language of beats, raps, or tilts. A name given to a kind of spirit communication system using beats or other noises. Alphabetical typology is the designation of letters (or ciphers) by raps or tilts.

Trance — an expanded state of consciousness, characterized externally by apparent sleep or unconsciousness. During a trance, the medium may willingly serve as an instrument for a spirit communication.

Transitional Worlds — way stations that serve as resting places for free spirits.

Trial — a life or state of pain or anguish that tests patience, endurance, courage, or belief. In the Spiritist literature, two other conditions are discussed: life of expiation in which the spirit repairs the wrong or harm done in a previous life, and life of mission, in which the spirit is assigned a task that impacts the social, cultural, spiritual, scientific, or artistic components of a group or society.

Vital Principle — the principle that gives organic life to all beings; it has its source in the cosmic principle.

Vitalism — the theory that life processes arise from, or contain, a non material vital principle and cannot be explained entirely as physical and chemical phenomena. The vitalist concept is at the heart of the Spiritist view of the origin of life. Christian Spiritism maintains that this vital force has its origin in God, the Divine Source, the First Cause of all things, and that life is not solely the result of biochemical processes and organic evolution.

CONTENT INDEX

For information on other works by Allan Kardec, or to start or join a study group, write to:

ALLAN KARDEC EDUCATIONAL SOCIETY
P.O. Box 26336
Philadelphia, PA 19141
Phone (215) 329-4010

Or

AKES—BOOK DISTRIBUTION CENTER
P.O. Box 30692
Phoenix, AZ 85046
Phone (602) 996-3123

Or visit our Web site:
WWW.ALLAN-KARDEC.ORG
e-mail: akesbooks@cox.net